E Q U A L I Z E R
Leadership in Action

**Equalization and Future Success
Through
Leadership in Action**

Angela J. Farlow

Library of Congress
Control Number: 2005901910

ISBN 0-9766758-0-3

First Printing ● 2005

Additional copies of this book are available by mail.
Send $ 29.95 (includes tax and postage) to:
ELIA
P.O. BOX 477
Copperas Cove, Texas 76522
(254) 542-4195

Published by Angela J. Farlow

Printed in the USA by
Morris Publishing
3212 E. Hwy 30
Kearney, NE 68847

# Contents

## Dreams

A dream is a visual image of the future, how the future might be, or how the future could be. *The dream remains simply a dream without an individual taking action and remaining steadfast until the dream becomes reality.* Premature ending of efforts employed by an individual as he/she has tried to reach a desired outcome is what I refer to as *dream degradation.* I believe that dream degradation is one of the primary results for underachievement, individual lack of motivation, overloaded prison systems, and other situations defined by mainstream society as undesirable. Avoiding the possibility of dream degradation, public education systems can be a method of effective intervention. Public education systems have the ability to ensure that students experience their dreams becoming reality.

As the nation continues to undergo the pains of unprecedented change, issues of accountability in the public education system becomes even more pressing. Administrators, educators, parents, members of the community, national, state, and local policy makers have all became more actively involved in research-based educational explorations. They are seeking methods of instruction and/or intervention mechanisms that will ensure student academic achievement and success. A combination of these same beliefs, personal experiences, and dreams for the future is how the Equalizer: Leadership in Action (ELIA) Project and a new definition of leadership has evolved. The intent of this book is to provide educational stakeholders with real world examples and tools necessary to effectively increase student awareness about the need to become receptive of a quality education. Resulting in the effective implementation of the ELIA Project are students who strive to achieve excellence in a variety of environments for a lifetime.

## About the Book

Readers will learn about the powerful effects of the student leadership training. This book is a combination of the author's personal experiences, methods of student leadership development, student accountability, responsibility, achieving educational ownership, true empowerment, and research. It also includes the various perspectives of the author as a former teacher at C. E. Ellison High School and current Senior Class Administrator at the Copperas Cove High School located in Copperas Cove, Texas. Although the book includes student research studies, it has a format that is easy to read, understood, and lessons for a variety of readers (student, parents, teachers, administrators, educational leaders, policy makers, community leaders, businesses, media, and college or university professors). Some of the stories included are those written by students, faculty members, members of the Board of Directors, and parents all referencing student leadership development or specific experiences from varying perspectives. The Equalizer: Leadership in Action prepares its readers to experience a paradigm shift about public education, current public education reform movements, and about high school student's capabilities to take the necessary actions to promote effective changes in their environments.

## Book Format

The Equalizer: Leadership in Action format has four main sections. In the first section, a series of scenarios will allow reader participation and simulated decision-making. Readers can then compare their selected choices with those of the author's detailed actual experiences. The second section consists of examining a realistic and practical theory that provides public school systems with answers focused on accomplishing school, district, and state guidelines for student learning, achievement, and success. Additionally, the book includes methods of motivating students to become committed to achievement and success, lifelong learners, and actively exercising their abilities to influence both their internal and external environments. The third section provides research and examples of student leadership development methods tried, tested, and successful in a public school setting. A final section includes the Model of Excellence divided into eight phases for successful implementation. Also found in this section are some of the components of the Farlow Instrument Package 2004 (FIP-2004). The FIP-2004 is a set of tools that accurately assesses high school student leadership development and the components of an effective high school leadership program according to federal guidelines. The overall development of this book's intent is to serve as an aid to public schools as they address the following:

❖ An effective method to "Close The Gap" between student academic achievement linked to ethnic, cultural, social, economic, gender and/or environmental differences;

❖ An effective method that ensures that no child is left behind through the identification of student leaders and students gifted and talented in leadership;

❖ Use of a set of tools that provide stated goal achievement data and measures;

❖ Modeled use of the 11 components of comprehensive school reform (CSR) stimulating school, district, and state-wide reforms;

❖ Effective classroom management and assistance for individuals new to the teaching profession, and

❖ Student attendance and drop out rates.

## Special Thanks

To my husband Charles who continually gave words of encouragement and managed all aspects of our household as I completed this book project. He was there as a friend, sounding board, and patient advocate throughout the process.

To my children, DeAngela and Charles, whose pride in their mother gave me the courage to continue writing about a topic that is not widely understood or supported by others.

To my students and their parents who gave support, input, and witnessed the difficulty of taking on such a task. They saw this as my ability to give them the recognition that they deserved.

To the many others who either directly or indirectly provided me with the fire to ensure that my words and ideas about the future were heard.

ELIA

# Scenario Instructions

## Scenario Introduction

Each scenario begins with an introduction that includes conversations and the details for a specific situation. Within the introduction portion of the scenario, the reader asked to become Angela at different stages in her life. While considering the culture, environmental factors, and specific events in the life of Angela, the reader is will make the best decision with limited information based on each scenario's possible consequences. The reader's task is to make his/her decision based on Angela's ability to survive each circumstance trying to anticipate her mother's reaction about her decision selection. The purpose of these simulations is to allow the reader to get an idea about the origins of my passion and optimistic ideas for the nation's future direction of public school systems. Each simulation has several choices and the reader should not be concerned about making a wrong decision. There is no wrong decision. Readers should attempt to keep their minds open and the possibly of personal paradigm shift in regards to the various environments some of today's youth are surviving in.

# Scenario Activity

This section's design to allow the reader to experience the full impact of his/her decision made as Angela. The reader will need to locate a cover sheet and cover the entire flowchart, diagram, or table before continuing. The reader follows only his/her selected path until reaching the end of the activity. After completing the scenario activity, the reader should compare his/her decision with the other available choices. Each reader should take a moment to reflect about the situation in the scenario, make self-comparisons, and note any perceptual changes. Readers need to think about the following questions:

❖ Is leadership development dependent upon one's age?
❖ Does the environment play a role in leadership development?
❖ Can environmental conditions influence an individual's ability to make good decisions and choices?
❖ Would the majority of children at the same stage of development have the ability to complete similar tasks given similar environmental situations?

# Discussion

Remembering that you are still role-playing as Angela, explain how Angela feels before, during, and after the decision that she just made. After completing the discussion section, think about Maslow's Hierarchy of Basic Needs and decide if Angela's needs are met.

## Actual Events

In this section, the reader should compare his/her decision to those of the actual event. Reflect.

Scenario Activity Cover Sheet
Cut this sheet along the line

# Chapter 1 – Big Sister

**Scenario #1**

E L.
A

Angela is a five-year-old African American girl. She never knew her biological father and only learned his first name through a conversation with her grandmother. She said, "he was a no good scoundrel." Her two-year-old brother's father had a similar end. Her mother was the oldest child in the father's (Angela's grandfather) first family of 11 children, and she was responsible for taking care of her younger siblings. The mother never played with dolls as a child because there were always real babies needing real diapers to be changed and real mouths fed. Angela often lived with her grandmother when the grandmother learned about details of the lifestyle choices of the mother of her grandchildren. The move was often without Angela's younger brother because he liked to play with fire. Two of the grandmother's homes had already been lost to fires. Angela did not see her grandfather often because after eleven children (seven single birth pregnancies and two resulting in twins) he divorced her grandmother. He soon remarried a woman who was approximately the same age as his oldest daughter, and together they had eight children. Angela's mother stated that she felt her family was better off once her father had left.

You are Angela. You have just awoken from a nap. Unable to tell time you look at the hands on the clock. They have passed the mark that your mother made so that you would know when she would be home to fix your lunch. There is no telephone in the home. You turn on the television and realize that it is showing a program that comes on after you have normally eaten lunch. Soon your little brother wakes up and wanders to your location. Silently, you both sit and wait for your mother to come home so that you can eat lunch. Your little brother states that he is hungry. You already know this is true because your hunger pains have now reached high up beneath your ribs and low down into your stomach causing it to twist and turn. You look at the clock again. Becoming weak, nervous, and shaky from hunger, you search the refrigerator shelves only to find uncooked bacon and eggs. At a distance, you hear the sound of a car door shut. You peek out of the window and notice your neighbor walking into her house. What decision does Angela make as a five-year-old?

## Decision/Consequences

Please cover the entire flowchart with the provided cover sheet before continuing the activity. Once the flowchart is covered, continue to read by sliding the paper down just enough to allow you to read only one section at a time starting at the very top of the diagram. After the decision point, where the reader makes his/her choice, follow the arrows based on your number 1 or 2 [Yes] or 3 [No] consequence choice. Compare the choice that Angela made based on the chosen consequence with the other available choices. Later, compare the decision made at this point with the actual event.

## Start

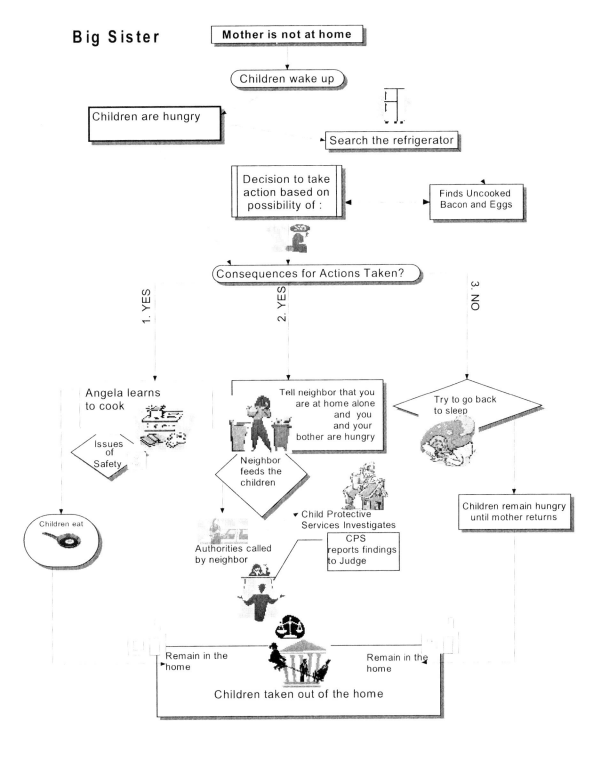

Big Sister

Mother is not at home

Children wake up

Children are hungry

Search the refrigerator

Decision to take action based on possibility of :

Finds Uncooked Bacon and Eggs

Consequences for Actions Taken?

1. YES

2. YES

3. NO

Angela learns to cook

Issues of Safety

Children eat

Tell neighbor that you are at home alone and you and your bother are hungry

Neighbor feeds the children

Try to go back to sleep

Children remain hungry until mother returns

Child Protective Services Investigates

CPS reports findings to Judge

Authorities called by neighbor

Remain in the home

Remain in the home

Children taken out of the home

5

# Discussion

1. Express Angela's anticipated view of how her mother will feel when she returns home.
2. Can you suggest two reasons that Angela has this anticipated view of how her mother will feel?
3. How does Angela feel about her ability to be responsible for herself and her brother based on the choice selected?
4. Suggest some ways that Angela may express her experiences and feeling as an adult or pre-teen.
5. Would it be safe to assume that there might be behavioral and/or emotional evidence based on these feelings? Explain.

# Actual Events

Hunger sensations signaled the need to begin scooting the aluminum-framed chair across the kitchen floor and push its back up against the cabinet. Becoming weak, nervous, and shaky from hunger, I searched the refrigerator shelves and found something that was manageable. I pushed the bacon and eggs onto the top of the cabinet and climbed into the seat of the chair so that I could reach everything. My brother entered into the kitchen and asked what I was doing. He asked, "Where's momma? I'm hungry." I told him that she was still at work. "What are you doing? You're going to be in trouble for being up there messing with that stuff." I explained to my brother that I was only going to use a little food so that momma would not be mad. I had watched momma plenty of times as I stood up in the chair and washed dishes and cleaned the cabinet tops as she cooked. I remembered that momma said to always keep the area clean while cooking. I filled the sink about half way with water and dishwashing liquid so that I could clean up any messes that I made while cooking. While standing high above the floor in the chair, I grabbed the cord to the electric skillet and plugged it in. I turned the dial two marks above low and waited for it to become warm to the touch.

While the skillet was warming, I carefully separated bacon into long strips discovering that bacon was stretchable. I laid the bacon strips in the center of the electric skillet. I turned the skillet temperature to low, and I watched the meat as the slow bubbles moved the meat up and down. Sounds of frying, bubbles popping as they formed around the bacon strips, and a pretty reddish brown color underneath signaled that it was time to put on my armor so that I could turn the bacon strips over. I armed myself with a long potholder that reached up to my armpit. Grabbing the spatula with my protected hand, I carefully turned the strips of bacon over. I then discovered that as bacon cooked, it was no longer stretchy.

After removing the bacon strips from the skillet, I cracked two eggs. I remembered the big splashes that the dishwater would make when I tossed a cup into it. I could not take a chance for the hot oil to splash like that, so I released the eggs close to the bottom of the skillet. Each of the eggs dropped out of their shells and settled into their places in the skillet. I tried to turn the eggs over as I had seen my mother do many times, but the eggs stuck to the spatula and the yellow yoke made their design on the bottom of the skillet. I just let them stay in place until I did not see any more runny yoke seeping out of the sides. As the eggs started to become less runny and started to puff up, I remembered that momma used different seasonings in the food. I was not sure which ones momma had used. I had just seen her shaking stuff into the foods that she cooked. I opened several containers, looked in the bottles, and selected the seasonings according to smell. Some seasonings tickled my nose and caused me to sneeze and others smelled good. I selected seasonings that made the eggs turn a pretty color. The aroma of the bacon and eggs danced around my nose.

As we sat at the kitchen table and ate, my brother told me that he liked it. I tasted it and he was right. I thought, "my first cooked meal is good so I am a good cook." That made me very proud. I was excited and eager to share my new skill with my mother when she came home. That evening I told my mother that I knew how to cook, and she did not believe me. I wanted to prove it to her, so I asked if I could cook dinner to prove it. She agreed and stood in the kitchen and watched me as I prepared everything to go through my cooking routine. When it came to the eggs, my mother came over and showed me how to flip them over so that the egg yolks would not bust. I gently splashed the oil on top of the eggs as they fried. After a few minutes, I flipped the eggs over for the other side to cook. That night, we all ate bacon, eggs, and toast for dinner. At that moment, I realized that we did not have to wait for momma to come home before we could eat anymore. That day marked the beginning of me cooking when we were hungry.

## Discussion

1. Express Angela's anticipated view of how her mother will feel when she returns home.
2. Can you suggest two reasons that Angela has this anticipated view of how her mother will feel?
3. How does Angela feel about her ability to be responsible for herself and her brother based on the choice selected?
4. Suggest some ways that Angela may express her experiences and feeling as an adult or pre-teen.

5. Would it be safe to assume that there might be behavioral and/or emotional evidence based on these feelings? Explain.

## Actual Events

Hunger sensations signaled the need to begin scooting the aluminum-framed chair across the kitchen floor and push its back up against the cabinet. Becoming weak, nervous, and shaky from hunger, I searched the refrigerator shelves and found something that was manageable. I pushed the bacon and eggs onto the top of the cabinet and climbed into the seat of the chair so that I could reach everything. My brother entered into the kitchen and asked what I was doing. He asked, "Where's momma? I'm hungry." I told him that she was still at work. "What are you doing? You're going to be in trouble for being up there messing with that stuff." I explained to my brother that I was only going to use a little food so that momma would not be mad. I had watched momma plenty of times as I stood up in the chair and washed dishes and cleaned the cabinet tops as she cooked. I remembered that momma said to always keep the area clean while cooking. I filled the sink about half way with water and dishwashing liquid so that I could clean up any messes that I made while cooking. While standing high above the floor in the chair, I grabbed the cord to the electric skillet and plugged it in. I turned the dial two marks above low and waited for it to become warm to the touch.

While the skillet was warming, I carefully separated bacon into long strips discovering that bacon is stretchable. I laid the bacon strips in the center of the electric skillet. I turned the skillet temperature to low, and I watched the meat as the slow bubbles moved the meat up and down. Sounds of frying, bubbles popping as they formed around the bacon strips, and a pretty reddish brown color underneath signaled that it was time to put on my armor so that I could turn the bacon strips over. I armed myself with a long potholder that reached up to my armpit. Grabbing the spatula with my protected hand, I carefully turned the strips of bacon over. I then discovered that as bacon cooked, it was no longer stretchy.

After removing the bacon strips from the skillet, I cracked two eggs. I remembered the big splashes that the dishwater would make when I tossed a cup into it. I could not take a chance for the hot oil to splash like that, so I released the eggs close to the bottom of the skillet. Each of the eggs dropped out of their shells and settled into their places in the skillet. I tried to turn the eggs over as I had seen my mother do many times, but the eggs stuck to the spatula and the yellow yoke made their design on the bottom of the skillet. I just let them stay in place until I did not see any more runny yoke seeping out of the sides. As the eggs started to become less runny and started to puff up, I remembered that momma used different seasonings in the food. I was not sure which ones momma had used. I had just seen her shaking stuff into the foods that she cooked. I opened several containers, looked in the bottles, and selected the seasonings according to smell. Some seasonings tickled my nose and caused me to sneeze and others smelled good. I selected seasonings that made the eggs turn a pretty color. The aroma of the bacon and eggs danced around my nose.

As we sat at the kitchen table and ate, my brother told me that he liked it. I tasted it and he was right. I thought, "my first cooked meal is good so I am a good cook." That made me very proud. I was excited and eager to share my new skill with my mother when she came home. That evening I told my mother that I knew how to cook, and she did not believe me. I wanted to prove it to her, so I asked if I could cook dinner to prove it. She agreed and stood in the kitchen and watched me as I prepared everything to go through my cooking routine. When it came to the eggs, my mother came over and showed me how to flip them over so that the egg yolks would not bust. I gently splashed the oil on top of the eggs as they fried. After a few minutes, I flipped the eggs over for the other side to cook. That night, we all ate bacon, eggs, and toast for dinner. At that moment, I realized that we did not have to wait for momma to come home before we could eat anymore. That day marked the beginning of me cooking when we were hungry.

# Chapter 2 – Skinny Little Tattle Tale

**Scenario #2**

Angela's mom and her friends have just left going out to party all night. Angela's mom has taken you and your little brother over to her friend's house. You do not talk much because you are an active listener when the adults talk. Your mother's friend's teenaged daughter is supposed to baby sit you while they are out. Angela and her little brother sit quietly next to one another and watch television. The teenaged girl's friends start coming over and they all go back into the girl's room. The sounds of giggling and smell of perfume diffusing through the air signals to you know that they are getting ready for something. Soon, the girls emerge with make up on and making final adjustments to one another clothes and hair. The girls all comment about how cute and well behaved to two of you are.

This is the second time that Angela's mother has left her and her little brother for the teenaged girl to baby sit. The first time resulted in a frightening experience for Angela while her little brother played in another room and she was left alone with the teenaged girl's older brother. You are Angela panicked because you realize that the teenaged girl and her friends are about to leave you in the same situation as before. You glance over at the older brother, and he just smiles at you. You feel your heart begin to race and almost pound its way out of your chest. The door opens and the girls begin to file out. Watching the girls' leave and the boy still smiling, Angela releases a terrifying scream. The scream startles the girls, and they come back into the house to investigate its cause. The girls surround you asking questions, "What's wrong? Are you scared? Do you want us to go and find your momma? What action does Angela take?

## Decision/Consequences

Please cover the entire table with the provided cover sheet before continuing. Once the table is covered, slide the paper to the left uncovering the column number 1-3 only. After reading the, *tells reason for scream* choices, slide the paper to the left again and read only the second column. Select either row one, two, or three and read the outcome column for the selection. Compare your choice with other available choices. How did the selected choice affect Angela?

# Skinny Little Tattle Tale

| Angela tells reason for scream | Intermediate Outcome | Final Outcome |
|---|---|---|
| 1. Baby sitter's brother hits her. | Baby sitter tells older brother not to hit the children. | Brother no longer hits the children. |
| 2. Angela fears being left alone. | Baby sitter assures Angela that older brother will protect them. | Children enjoy their Stay. |
| 3. Angela fears Babysitter's brother's games. | Baby sitter's brother wants to play house and doctor games. | Baby sitter remains in home to protect Angela. |

## Discussion

1. How did Angela feel about having a baby sitter?
2. Why did Angela feel panicked once she received the signal that the teenaged girl would be leaving soon?
3. How did Angela feel about the teenaged girls comments about her behavior?
4. What did the teenaged brother's smile mean to Angela?
5. After the letting out the big scream, how did Angela feel about explaining her scream?

## Actual Events

As a young child, I did not have the luxury of waiting for things to happen. I had developed the skill of knowing how to anticipate situations based on what could, or was likely to occur in my environment. I had also learned that by not being afraid to speak up about certain situations that I was contributing to my own safety and ability to remain as an untainted child. I actually liked it better and felt safer when my brother and I were at home together regardless of the length of time alone. I definitely liked this situation better than going over to other people's houses. She would often think that she was leaving us with her friend's teen-aged daughter to baby sit. In reality, the teen-aged baby sitter would often leave with other girls as soon our mother's had left. They were all going out to parties that lasted until the early morning hours.

One particular teen-aged boy saw me being left in the home as an opportunity to play house or doctor with a little girl who did not know any better.

However, I was no ordinary little girl. I would fight at the drop of a hat, and I was not afraid say that I would tell my mother about the boy's games that he wanted me to play. One time, as the boy's sister and her friends were about to leave, and I told her that I wanted to go with them. Laughing she said, "Oh baby, were going a place where little kids are not allowed". She and her friends exchanged comments about how cute and well mannered my brother and I were.

As the girls walked out of the door, leaving me under the care of her older brother, I released a powerful scream and began to cry. I screamed at the top of my voice that I did not want to be alone with her brother. The girls rushed back inside and started asking me questions about what was wrong. Nothing was wrong unless they left me there with her brother, and then something would be wrong. I would constantly have to scratch, slap, bite, and fight him to stay away from me. To stop him from trying to kiss on me as he tried to hold my small struggling arms, legs, and feet still. Finally, one of the friends asked me why I did not want to stay with the boy. Finally, I thought. Someone finally had asked the right question. Still crying, I screamed out, "Because he is always trying to kiss me and wants me to play nasty games with him".

In great surprise and disgust, the boy's sister and her friends started calling him a pervert. The sister and her friends starting beating him and he screamed, "she's lying! I would not do that". The girls did believe me because they continued to beat on him for a while. The sister then assured me that he would bother me again like that, and the girls all went out anyway. After the girls had left, the boy was still very angry and embarrassed. He said that he was only joking with my skinny little ass. He also told me that I had a big mouth and called me a skinny little tattletale. I did not care what he said or called me as long as he left me alone and kept his distance away from me. I never did tell my mother about the incident, because the issue had been resolved. I always suspected that the teenaged girl had not told her mother either because she was not supposed to have left the house.

12

# Chapter 3 – New School Clothes

**Scenario #3**

**E**L. **L**A. It is a hot summer day, and Angela's mother is having one of her crying spells. Whenever her mother was having a day like this, Angela makes sure that her and her brother did not do anything to make her feel worse. They remained very quiet. They would just sit on the couch and only moved their mouths having entire conversations or they would use their predetermined sign language. Angela had to quickly learn to identify differences in her mother's behavior by her frustrations as a mother, too much partying, or when the behavior was from being too tired. Today seems very different to Angela. Angela wonders if her mother is crying because she has done something wrong. Finally, she hears, "Angela, come here baby". She likes it when her mother calls her baby because that means that she has not done anything wrong and will not be in trouble.

Angela walks into her mother's bedroom and sits on the edge of her bed rubbing her mother's forehead to make her feel better. You are Angela. As you sit on the edge of the bed still caressing your mother's forehead, you ask your mother what is wrong. Your mother then sits up in bed and tells you that she needs you to be a big girl for her. She explains that she needs your help. She wants you to take care of your two-year old brother while she is at work. She warns you about the nosey neighbors and the mother states that no one can know that you and your brother are in the house. She also tells you that that if you do a good job caring for your brother that she will pay you for babysitting him. You are to save the money to buy your new clothes for kindergarten at the end of the summer. Realizing that your mother needs your help, you state, "Momma, my goodness, is that all you were crying about? Huh, I can take real good care of my little brother". The prospect of buying your own new clothes for kindergarten sounds like a great reward to you.

After listening to all of your mother's endless prompts and examples about what could go wrong, the only thing concerning you is starting kindergarten with new pretty clothes. The next morning you wake up, and it is the first day of your new mission. You will take care of your little brother all day while your mother is at work. As you prepare cereal and toast for breakfast, your thoughts wander off and you picture yourself as being a big girl by doing a real good job. A real good job that might even result in getting some new shoes, hair ribbons, and bows to match. Maybe even some new big girl panties. The statement, "Take care of..." to some individuals might be defined as play with, share things with, or other child-like activities, but to you, take care of means to bathe, feed, and not to let out of your sight. Once breakfast is on the table, you go and wake your brother up so that you

13

can wash his face and hands for breakfast. While washing your brother's face and hands, you tell him that he has to be good and mind you just, as he has to mind momma because you are the oldest. Your little brother agrees.

After breakfast, you wash the morning dishes and start getting your little brother ready for his bath. Your little brother starts to cry and say that he is cold. Afraid that he will catch a cold or get sick, you wrap him up in a towel and adjust the water to a warm temperature for his bath. He is still shivering, you glance over at the little stove in the bathroom. What action does Angela take?

## Decision/Consequences

Please cover the entire flowchart with the provided cover sheet before continuing the activity. Once the flowchart has been covered, start at the very top of the diagram, continue the activity by sliding the paper down just enough to allow you to read the *Does Angela try to complete the task* section. Here, you must make a decision, follow the arrows based on your decision of 1 or 2 [Yes], or 3 [No]. Follow your selected path and continue reading until you arrive at the stop sign ending the activity. At this point, compare the decision that Angela made with the other available choices. How did the selected choice of decision affect Angela? Later, compare the decision made at this point with the actual event.

**Start**

# *New School Clothes*

Mother's instructions◄

Does Angela try to complete the task?

1. YES

2. YES

3. NO

Danger!

Mother saves money?

Mother save money?

NO

New School Clothes?

NO

STOP

NO

YES

EXPLOSION

NO

New School Clothes?

STOP

Angela is successful babysitting brother

YES

New School Clothes?

The End

# Discussion

1. How might a child coming from this type of environment view authority? Explain.
2. What gave Angela the belief that she could complete her mother's request?
3. Did Angela's mother seem to doubt her ability to take care of her younger brother while she worked? Provide two justifications for your answer.
4. How would a child coming from this type of environment view his/her ability to accomplish tasks in a new environment?
5. Can having knowledge about an individual's environment assist others relate to their own type of environment? Explain.

# Actual Events

Wow! Babysitting my brother all day while my mother was at work was going to be a new experience. My brother was still crying because he was cold, so I decided that I would make a big girl decision. I decided that I was going to turn on the little stove in the bathroom. I was a little nervous, but I had seen my mother do it plenty of times. I turned the knob, but nothing happened. Suddenly, I remembered that my mother had to use a match to make the fire stay on. As my little brother continued to cry, I ran into the kitchen and got some matches. I knew that I would be in big trouble if I played with matches, but I was not playing with them. I just needed to use them to light the bathroom stove.

When I returned, my brother was still crying and whimpering. I told him that he had to be quiet and stop crying because this was dangerous and I could be "burned up". When I turned to check on him, he stood there with the towel between his teeth quietly whimpering. I nervously smiled at him, and I told him that would tell momma what a good little brother he had been. He nodded his head that he agreed and whimpered even more quietly. With my fingers and palms beginning to sweat from fear, I took a match out of the box and scrapped it along the edge of the box. This was another new experience. I lit the match, but I was afraid to put it close to the little stove. It had a "stinky smell" and it was making a hissing sound. I blew out the match and I quickly turned the knob the other way. I waited for the smell to go away. My little brother started to cry again saying that he was cold. I was so nervous that my armpits itched, sweat rolled down my forehead, and I nervously popped every one of my knuckles.

I took a deep breath and turned the knob again. This time I would not turn it as much so that the sound would not be so scary and it would not stink up the bathroom so bad. This time I had a plan. I was afraid that I that the flame would come out so far that it would reach out and burn me. At that moment, I

16

remembered my mother and her friends talking about stove accidents. I remembered hearing them describe the agonizing pain that little children had to endure from fire accidents. Some of their stories ended with the child surviving, but some of them did not. I thought to myself, "If I got all burned up, I will not be able to get my new school clothes."

With those thoughts in mind, I had to make sure that my brother was at a safe distance away from the stove, in case the flame jumped out. I told him to stand outside of the bathroom door and wait until I called him. He left the bathroom. This time I turned the knob just a little bit, stood back, scraped the match against the edge of the box, and threw it into the little stove. The fire stayed on but it started to sputter. I turned the knob a little more until I could feel the heat against my face. I slowly turned the knob the other way until the flame became smaller. Soon it stopped popping and sputtering. As I leaned down to pick up the graveyard of matches scattered around on the floor, I noticed that the bathroom rug had a small scorched area on it. I thought, "I probably won't get a whooping if I tell momma before she finds it herself." I decided that I would meet her at the door and tell on myself before she went into the bathroom. I shouted "Yeah, the fire stayed on" and called my little brother into the bathroom to give him his bath. We both celebrated the victory by clapping, singing, and dancing around.

I was so proud of what I had accomplished. I could hardly wait until I my mother got home, so that I could tell her about the day's events. After bathing my brother, I got him dressed and I got ready for my own bath. I told my brother to go and bring some of his toys into the bathroom so that I could watch him while I finished my bath. After getting dressed, we completed our daily chores, took a nap played the rest of the day. I took the responsibility as keeper of the house and of my little brother very seriously. Motivating factors to complete all tasks dependably was an effort to let my mother know that she could depend on me. I also wanted to show her that I could be a big girl in her absence.

This was the highlight of my summer before kindergarten with one exception. When I finally had the opportunity to share my victory with my mother, she simply said, "Baby, you do not turn that stove on during the summer. Do not do that again," and she went back to sleep. When I started going to kindergarten, I was able to wear my new pretty dresses, ribbons, big girl panties, and shoes. At times, I was a little embarrassed when the other children at school talked about what their mothers and fathers did with or for them. I was not able to share stories like those.

I learned to rely on some of my teachers and others for the support that allowed me to develop into who I am today. Some of my teachers made me feel special when they told tell me that I looked nice. I can still remember the good

17

feeling that I experienced when my music teacher told me that I was a very talented and very determined little girl. She stated, "Angela, I believe that you are capable of doing anything that you develop the determination to accomplish as long as you continue to learn and believe in your dreams. Never be afraid to trust in the willingness of others to help you get to your destiny." She told me to always remember what she had just told me, and I have. Still remembering her powerful words, I pass this same belief on to my students and others.

# Chapter 4 – Keeping the Promise

**ELA.** Angela has a developed keen sense of what is right and wrong from a very early age. She has developed the idea that she and her brother are well beyond disciplining as small children. She believes that she is a little miniature adult because she is often responsible for being on her own and making real-world decisions. At the age of nine, her mother met a man that she liked a lot. The mother asked Angela and her brother if they liked him. The children thought that he seemed nice enough, and in a way they welcomed the idea of being able to get know one of their mother's male friends. Before the mother actually married "the man", he had to teach her about the things that were to come during their marriage. That is all Angela ever called him at first, "the man".

One night "the man" and their mother went out together in a very happy mood, but when they returned, Angela heard her mother screaming and crying. She and her brother jump out of their beds and run to see what is happening. As they reached their mother's bedroom, they both witness "the man" hitting their mother. Angela and her brother start to cry and scream telling, "the man" to stop hitting their mother. He turns and screams, "Ya'll better get out of here!" The children are both afraid because "the man" is big and his face is expressing so much anger. Angela becomes so scared that she is sick to her stomach. While she is still crying and scared crazy, out of somewhere within her tiny body, words screamed out of her mouth, "If you hit my momma one more time I'm going to call the police. You are a drunk and I'll tell the police to put you in jail, and you need to go to jail!"

No telephone in the home, "the man" realizes that Angela will have to leave the house to make good on her promise. "The man" stops hitting the mother for a moment. He turns and looks directly at Angela and hit her mother again. It almost seems as if he wants to see what she will do. Angela screams, "Now you're going to jail." She turns and runs to the front door. Before she can even unlock the door, the man releases her mother. The mother comes out of the room and calls for Angela not to go. Angela stops. She looks at "the man" and then at her mother. With swollen, red, and tearing eyes, her mother says, "Everything is okay now." Still crying, and scared, Angela points up at the man and tells her mother, "No its not momma, because he's still here! Tell him to leave momma! I hate him! We don't need him to stay here with us momma!"

Standing in the doorway, "the man" stands nearby looking down at Angela and just listens. All of a sudden, big "crocodile tears" rolls down the man's cheeks. He says that he is very sorry that he hit our mother. He apologizes. He explains that he only acts like that because he loves the mother so much. "Yea, right, Angela thinks to herself. He looked at Angela and her brother and said that he was sorry.

19

He states that he loves both of them very much. The mother and brother may believe him, but Angela does not, and she tells him that.

About two weeks later, they married. Angela tells her mother that she wants to go and live with her grandmother. The man said that we are a family now and that he wants us to all be together. After a few days, the grandmother stops by, and Angela tells her what happened. The grandmother asked Angela's mother if the children could come and live with her. She said that children do not need to see that kind of stuff going on. Unknown to their grandmother, Angela and her brother were used to seeing a lot of stuff going on at our house.

You are Angela. Angela has always been her brother's protector, and she is determined not to let that change no matter who is around. One day, your brother does something that makes "the man" angry. He whoops your brother. Your brother's pleas and screams sound like he the beating is killing him. As he is whooping your brother, you run into the living room and tell your mother to do something. Your mother just sits there in silence on the couch shaking her head no. You cannot believe that your mother is not going to do anything about her son being beat "half to death". You hate her for that. Soon your brother comes through the living room on his way to the bedroom. It sounds like he can hardly breathe. Your mother has whooped both of you before, but not like that.

As your brother continued to walk and gets near you, you go over to him and put your arms around him as you both walk into the bedroom. Sitting on your brother's bed, you promise him that the next time, you will do something. He asks you, "What?" You can only reply, "I don't know yet. Just try to stay away from him and don't make him mad." Your brother agrees. Your opportunity to do something comes sooner than you had anticipated. You wake up to the sounds of your brother's screams. You run into the living room, but no one is in there. You run into your mother's bedroom, and she and your stepfather are both sitting up in the bed. Your stepfather is demanding that your brother return to an original location so that he can reach him to hit him again. You notice that your stepfather is beating your brother with a brown extension cord. You can hear the cord whistle as he swings it to strike your brother again. The force from the strike causes your brother to stumble and lunge forward. You do not know what to do. What action does Angela take?

# *Keeping the Promise*

Angela runs into bedroom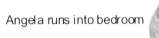

Angela witnesses her stepfather beating her brother

There are consequences for any action taken by Angela.
Based on the knowledge that you have gained about
Angela's environment, choose option #1,2, or 3 predicting the one that
most closely resembles the actual events.

OPTION #1

Children live with their
grandmother

OPTION #2

Angela calls the authorities

OPTION #3

Keeping the promise

## Discussion

1. Thinking about Angela's selected choice, how do you think her mother is affected?
2. How do you think other mothers in her neighborhood views Angela's mother?
3. Were other options available for Angela? If so, please explain.
4. In childhood, what type of relationship exists between Angela and her brother?
5. Explain how the relationship may change between Angela and her brother once they become adults.

## Actual Events

Finally, I shouted, "That's enough!" My stepfather looked at me in disbelief as I ran forward and snatched the end of the extension cord before it reached my brother again. Strengths unmatched, I continued to hold onto the end of the cord so tightly that my fingers became numb. Looking into my stepfather's eyes, I told my brother to move, and I stood there in his place. My mother just looked at me, surprised. My stepfather said, "Oh, so you must want you're ass whooped to, huh." I said, " No, but I am tired of you always beating on my brother." He snatched the cord from my hand, and swung it and hit me across my shoulder and arm. The pain shot through me, but I did not move, I just stood there and stared at him. He said, "Oh, so you think you are tough, huh." With that, he bit his bottom lip and swung the extension cord with even greater force to hit me again. This time, I caught the extension cord again with one hand. My hand was burning, but my adrenalin must have been elevated to new levels. The adrenalin was bursting through my little body out of fear, and the blood rushing through my veins felt hot. This time when he snatched back on the cord, I was able to hang on to it.

With tears silently rolling down my face, I repositioned myself as he continued to snatch back on the extension cord. I did not let go. He was snatching on the cord, and holding the cover over his lower body. I decided that he must have been naked underneath the covers, and I knew that he was not going to expose himself to me. Realizing this as an advantage, I stared into his eyes and continued to snatch, pull, and brace myself while still hanging onto the extension cord. Mother began to laugh as she watched us play tug-of-war. Finally, he said, "Take your crazy ass out of here." I could hear him tell my mother how crazy I was. He said, "Did you see that little fool. She was actually willing to take an ass whooping for her little bad assed brother. That little nigger is really crazy!"

I heard them both begin to laugh, but I did not see anything funny. I went into the bedroom and sat down on my bed. My brother soon came over and sat

22

beside me. He asked what had happened, and I showed him my red hand. I demonstrated that my hand was so sore that I could barely move my fingers. He thanked me for keeping the promise that I had made to him. I told him that we only had each other now since momma had sided with "the man". We both agreed. I started to like the idea that my stepfather thought that I was crazy. I decided that crazy meant that my behavior was unpredictable. Crazy also showed him that I was determined not to allow him to abuse my brother. Memory of this event served as a behavior gauge or guide to assist me as I accomplished future goals. A situation may be painful, but if you remain determined and committed to overcoming the pain, you will succeed.

## In Loving Memory

The included scenarios may seem harsh by some and even unimaginable by others, but I still hold loving memories about my mother. She passed away at the age of 54 on Thanksgiving Day in 1997. She had a massive heart attack. I still find myself wishing that she were still here, so that she can see that my brother and I are still okay. I would share with my mother, as I have shared with my readers, about how much I have benefited from the memories and experiences of my childhood. As a result, there are few things that I allow myself to believe that I cannot do simply because it may be a new concept or activity. I am always willing to try it. Failed attempts to accomplish a task, I approach simply as temporary obstacles that cause me to find a different method of approach.

Some individuals have viewed my actions as being stubborn acts or foolish pride. Instead of stubborn, I use the term determined. As for the foolish pride portion, I definitely do not believe in *beating my head against a brick wall*. First, that would be too painful, and next, I refuse to utilize energy just spinning my wheels and getting nowhere. I utilize my reflection skills, ability of self-knowledge, and the feedback and of others when determining if I am able to effectively complete a task. This does not mean that I give up easily. It just means that when it becomes evident that I am ineffective at an activity, or if I cannot see how the activity will benefit anyone, I weight my response or actions against choices that are available. If I have the choice to avoid a no win activity, without harming anyone, I discontinue my efforts. If the activity is a part of my direct responsibility, I complete the activity but continue to try to find a more effective way to complete the activity for the next time it arises. The attitude and ideas that I hold about live in general and about my ability to accomplish my dreams are both due to my childhood experiences and my perception about the lasting worth or benefits of those experiences.

I believe that my mother felt guilty later in life as she reflected about how she raised my brother and I. We do not blame our childhood experiences or believe that they stunted our growth as productive citizens. We simply view our childhood experiences as a product of circumstances and environmental influences that were beyond our mother's control. I feel that she did the best job in raising us that she knew how to do. I am thankful that I had many opportunities to express this view to her before it was too late.

## Section 2 – Leadership Theory Development

# Chapter 5 – Leadership Philosophy

## Childhood Views

E.L.A. If someone made the statement, "I had a unique childhood". A variety of individuals might unique answers for that question due to either positive or negative situations that were present in their childhood. Ruby Payne (1998) has stated that poverty is relative. It would be difficult to think, understand, or categorized as poor, or anything else, if everyone surrounding shared the same or similar situation. Differences, shortcomings, or blessings might even exist in the mind as the "norm" if never required to leave the environment of familiarity. Few would survive in an environment absent of human-to-human interaction. This means that at some stage, or point, we probably become aware of how others live, what they do, or at the very least, that they live differently than we do. This seems to be when the natural human curiosities become aroused. Numerous researchers have dedicated most, if not all of their adult lives trying to determine the advantages or disadvantages of environmental issues on individual's ability to become a successful adult.

One day during a graduate class discussion, I shared my philosophy about leadership development, "I believe that leadership development begins during early childhood based on an individual's environment." Leadership theorist and researchers may not agree with this statement, that is, unless they share a similar childhood experience that lend support to that statement. Making no claims to be the "know it all" in leadership research, theory, or its development, the only claim that I can make with certainty is that my childhood demanded that I exhibit the characteristics, skills, and development of "what ever it may be called" for my survival. To those of you who have dedicated years of research on the topic of leadership development, you are welcomed to disagree, and I will gladly leave that potentially endless area of debate up to you as the experts. I do not intend to step on anyone's toes by writing this book. However, I am willing to share some of my ideas and research experiences that support my belief about student leadership development. I am also adding a new definition of leadership into the "leadership pot" to simmer. I call my definition a real world definition of leadership.

The class that I referred to earlier consisted of adult educators who were participating in a Master of Education course. As I listened to the sounds of their gasps, and viewed their wide-eyed expressions, I became aware that my childhood had been a unique one. After that experience, I started to reflect on some of the situations, experiences, or people that influenced and helped to shape my life. A collection of childhood experiences, some of which would equate to child abuse or severe neglect by today's standards, and ideas about the future shaped the person that I am today. Right or wrong, child abuse, severe neglect, or not, I have always viewed my life long experiences as a preparatory course for what lies ahead in my future. Bennis (2003) has stated that childhood experiences serve as guides to leadership growth, and I could not agree more.

## Theoretical Perspective

Discussions that had taken place in the graduate class that I mentioned earlier caused me to wonder about some of my childhood experiences. I asked myself if other five year olds would have had the same end if given similar situations, circumstances, or environments. Finally, I decided to try to connect my experiences to specific words. I came up with three different words: self-efficacy, self-regulation, and intrinsic motivation. I chose these words because they defined the successful experiences of my childhood in the absence of parental supervision. At a young age, the combination of the word self-efficacy, self-regulation, and intrinsic motivation developed me into a self-directed learner. As such, I learned how to successfully play the "hand dealt" me. I learned to direct my efforts into various situations with the goal of achieving successful results. It is for this reason that I believe that the power to accomplish great things lies within self. Some individuals are unaware that they possess this power, but providing individuals with calculated experiences and opportunities will ensure its enlightenment.

These series of investigations enhanced my ability to enjoy my first year of teaching, become an effective chemistry teacher, and develop the awareness about how active observation and inquiry can help educators solve problems. Utilizing a variety of methods to investigate and solve problems throughout my teaching career has provided me with a solid foundation understanding what is necessary to motivate students who want to learn. I later developed the *Theoretical Model of Academic Excellence* to combine what I was learning, observing, and trying into something that would provide tangible results. Initially developed in 2003, I made the final modifications to the *Theoretical Model of Academic Excellence* in 2004, I finally settled on the name *Model of Excellence* (ME).

What is excellence? Excellence in the context of my research refers to an individual's desire for constant improvement. My use of the term academic excellence refers to and individual's desire to seek academic improvement. This is accomplished by challenging one's self to achieve his/her best, enrolling in rigorous and challenging courses such as, Advanced Placement (AP) and Pre-Advanced Placement (Pre-AP) classes, and an individual having the realization that the level of academic achievement lies within his/her perception for the need to be receptive of a quality education. In summary, academic excellence refers to students striving to achieve their best through their diligent efforts. Students who seek to achieve their goals of both of these definitions excellence soon discover that there is little room for underachievement to creep into their lives.

Based on several questions and observations, I was able to develop the goals and components of the ME to assist students as they took actions to make their dreams become reality. Components for student leadership development occur on specific levels. I refer to this as *purposeful* student leadership development, and I developed the ME to directly address specific research questions. Research questions that guided the development of the Model of Excellence are as follow:

1. Can high school students develop the skills of an effective leader?
2. Can a definition of leadership describe what high school students *do* resulting from their effective leadership development?
3. Will students become self-directed learners when empowered to experience increased levels of self-efficacy, self-regulation, and intrinsic motivation through community service-based projects and outcome-based leadership development?
4. Will the topics of leadership development and community service-based projects stimulate high school students to transfer their learning into other areas that assists them to achieve academic excellence?
5. What will you see to support the belief that high school students have developed into effective leaders?

The development of the Model of Excellence satisfies one of my long-term dreams for the future. My dream is to serve as an instrument of public education change for state and national educational leaders along with educational policy makers. The full establishment and implementation of student leadership development programs and continued student leadership development research within the public school systems provides these individuals with the information that is needed to accomplish these goals with long-term results. Through my research, I have already put the first spin on the wheel of achieving this dream. Most of the challenges or questions that at one time seemed difficult to answer are included through my research.

## Trying Something New

I have conducted action research on the topic of student leadership development in my regular classrooms to aid in student success and achievement since 1998. After grading few test scores, I was not satisfied with the passing percentage rates. Today, many students have to endure issues worst than those I experienced during my childhood. Many students hold jobs to help their families experience financial security. Some students in these types of environment will exhibit resilience on their own, by using positive and motivating self-talk, and/or by telling themselves that regardless of their current situation that they will rise above it. Most teachers would agree that in every class there is a minority population of high achievers. This may be due to a variety of things. I was not going to be guilty of sending out into the world, students who were satisfied failing, meeting the minimum requirements, or doing just enough to get by. I discussed my dissatisfaction with the test scores and overall failing percentages with my students.

I used the results of the test scores as my method to try something different. As a result, I began to use the concept of student leadership development. I have always believed that students or individuals in general must feel in control of his/her own behavior and of their own destiny to a certain extent. This system of belief removes the possibility of blaming others for individual choices that may lead to failure to accomplish specific goals. The only immediate goals that I allowed for the students in my classes, was for them to strive to achieve their best. If through studying and completing all assignments resulted in the student receiving a C, I explained that they had achieved their best in that particular situation. My strict belief in preparing both responsible and accountable students capable of achieving their academic best served as my guide throughout my teaching career. For example, I simply suggested actions for my students to take as a guarantee of successful performance in my classroom. I suggested that each student to commit 15 minutes daily reviewing the current day's chemistry notes, problems, lab results or discussions. I also stated that due to my dissatisfaction in their test score performance that each day my students returned to class, there was a real possibility that they would have a quiz.

I allowed students time to complain about the suggestions and have discussions among themselves. Although at the same time, realizing that I would not tolerate only a low percentage of my students passing tests and striving to achieve academic excellence or performing at their best in class. Some students made the conscious choice to take my suggestions seriously and studied for the required 15 minutes. Other students made the conscious choice to ignore my suggestions about the required 15 minutes of after school study time. The students' ability to come to class prepared to learn was in their own hands. This action removed the student's ability to place the blame for failure on any individual other than self. As promised and having created more work for myself, everyday the students knew to expect a quiz before learning any new information.

At first, the scores indicated an undesirable academic performance by my students. In my own dramatic fashion, I started telling the students that they needed to stop stealing from me everyday, and some students asked, "Stealing?" I accused them of stealing the 15 minutes that I had asked them for on a daily basis. Some students decided that I was just crazy enough to really believe that they were capable of stealing time from me. Other students soon realized that I really meant what I had said about the 15 minutes daily. Soon, they began coming to class earlier and standing out in the hallway in front of class, and I could hear them reviewing for their expected quiz. I made a big deal about any level of improvement, even if the score was still a failing score, I still bragged on the students. Eventually, even some of my lowest performing students began to improve. In all of my classes, I always took the time to teach leadership skills and explained to my students that through developing these skills they will all be able to reap the full benefits of a quality education. Soon, the students started to believe it to.

My tactics, experiences, and research have provided me with a blue print for student success. The implementation of student leadership development holds the key for public school systems seeking to improve upon student academic achievement and success. Students must experience a paradigm shift towards the task of receiving and accomplishing the goal of excellence in academic achievement (Covey, 1998). Green (2001) quotes Getzels and Guba (1957), "that an individual is likely to be the most effective when his/her needs and the task to be performed are at the highest level of compatibility". One focus of my research is to *change the student's perception* about the need to become receptive of a quality education. Rosenbaum (2004) stated, "Today, nearly all high school seniors believe that they are going to college and that bad grades won't stop them." To a certain extent, it will not. However, how likely is it that this type of student standards will allow them to complete college? I would suspect the odds of college completion are low when compared to students who have prepared themselves for college while in high school. My research focuses on providing students with the tools needed to become aware of how knowledge in one area will assist them in a variety of other settings. Soon students began to use these learned skills in a variety of environments and in their academic courses.

## Theory Addition

When I first began to implement the components of my theory in 1998, it almost seemed too simple. I then started to search for a method to develop a model that would provide a visual interpretation for my explanation about student learning. I began by developing the components of the *Theoretical Model of Academic Excellence* (TMAE) in 2003 while I attempted to complete the thesis option for the Master of Education degree. The TMAE was a combination my original theory about student responsibility and accountability and the goal of helping students achieve all of the variables that I believed would effect student academic achievement and success. Conducting thesis research, I began to search for instruments that were specific for measuring student leadership development. Most of the available instruments were for adult or post-secondary participant research. I wanted to find instruments that were specific to high school student leadership development.

After many phone calls to universities and sending out what seemed like hundreds of E-mails, they all seemed to have one thing in common; responses of well wishes for my quest. I soon realized that I still did not have the answer that I was seeking. I found that I was no closer to finding an instrument that measured high school student leadership development or all of the TMAE variables than when I first began my initial searches. In the absence of instruments to measure student leadership development and the TMAE variables, I decided to develop a few of my own instruments. I began using the components of the Comprehensive School Reform (CSR) Program which began in 1998 and was authorized as Title I, Part F of the Elementary and Secondary Education Act signed into law on January 8, 2002 (Texas Education Agency [TEA], 2002).

An adequate system of scoring that offered information about the *degree* to which the outlined standards and guidelines was met for new program intervention was absent in both of these documents. Due to this absence, I developed a standard score greater than or equal to 80%, which in the educational setting equates to an above average score. This would be a good start. I also planned to make program effectiveness comparisons using the changes that I had made during the redesign phase of the C.E. Ellison High School Leadership Academy. The instruments that I had designed using the Federal Guidelines for Comprehensive School Reform (CSR) (U.S. Department of Education [ed.gov]. (n.d.)), No Child Left Behind (NCLB) (U.S. Department of Education [ed.gov]. (2002)), and the current practices that I had developed for C.E. Ellison High School Leadership Academy's the goals and objectives included in the 2003-2004 Campus Improvement Plans (CIP) (Killeen Independent School District [KISD] (2003) to provide a realistic measure for the program's level of intervention. The title of my thesis was, *A high school leadership development program: Promoting student self-efficacy, self-regulation, and student intrinsic motivation to learn*. One of my committee members felt that this approach was moving away from my original thesis goals and objectives. Was it?

In addition measuring the C.E. Ellison High School Leadership Academy program's level of intervention, I also wanted to make a comparison of goal achievement using the vision and mission statements for the program. First, I considered the vision statement: *Ellison Academy Growing Leaders of Excellence*. I kept the vision statement in mind as I made changes and decisions that directly affected the members and the program as a whole. What evidence showed the program's vision accomplishment? I will not answer this question at this time, just remember this question while reading about the 2004 Project Symposium later in this section of the book, and then answer, "Was the programs vision accomplished?" Try to develop an answer about the program's mission accomplishment. The real answer to these questions is located in the C. E. Ellison High School Leadership Academy Members section of the book, but do not read it now.

## Change of Plans

In twelve months, I had already completed all of the required courses for the Masters of Education degree and Principal Certificate with a December graduation date. I added an additional semester for the sole purpose of completing the thesis option. Soon it was February and I wanted to graduate with the Masters of Education degree and Principal Certificate qualifying me for employment in a principal's position for the 2004-2005 school year. Two of my thesis committee members showed their support regardless of my decision about completing the thesis. Finally, after much agonizing debate with myself, I decided to graduate in August 2004 since I still was not satisfied with what I had found to be available. Dr. Harrison stated that she knew how passionate I was about high school student leadership development, and she suggested that I continue with the study even after my graduation.

The result of this change in plan is that I refused to believe that all of the hours and searches that I had conducted for the thesis would be in vain. I decided that I would use the instruments and ideas that I had developed while preparing to complete my thesis. I asked member's parents, Mr. Rainwater (C. E. Ellison High School Principal), and Dr. Charles Patterson (KISD Superintendent) for permission to continue my research. Once all permissions granted, I was now on a different mission. I began my research with the members of the C. E. Ellison High School Leadership Academy in the Principles of Leadership classes.

I started using student leadership development based on theory, skills, and application. I assigned special projects to members so that they could test, try, and refine their learned skills. Some of the special student project ideas and opportunities came from other teachers and staff at the school. For example, several librarians in the Killeen Independent School District had been planning for an author's visit in selected schools for months. I learned of the plans from the librarian, Mrs. Duvall. However, there was a small problem. The librarians were experiencing financing difficulties for his visit. C. E. Ellison High School Leadership Academy came to the rescue. I had a budget that would allow us to help, but the help came with one condition. The condition was that I would select members of the C. E. Ellison High School Leadership Academy to coordinate everything with the librarian's final approval. As a result, David Lubar, author of *Hidden Talents* visited our school, interacted with students during planned class sessions, we handed out the T-Shirts that we had professionally made with a picture of him and his cat on it, member coordinators wore special T-Shirts for identification, and members had catered lunch with David Lubar and their invited guest.

In addition to all of this, I also began to gauge the student's levels of self-efficacy, self-regulation, and intrinsic motivation increases and development. Additionally, I became curious to find out if these skills would lead my students into becoming self-directed learners by interacting with one another, me, and other professionals in specific fields. Again, my curiosity was aroused, I wanted to observe if the combination of all of these variables would lead students to strive to achieve academic excellence, or better yet, strive to achieve excellence in whatever they decided to become involved in. I also used some of the tools that I developed and called Farlow's Instrument Package –2004 (FIP-2004) to measure student leadership development and improvement. It began to appear as if these students were experiencing unequaled growth and progress when compared to students in other programs that existed within the school. These students were willing to take the steps that lead them to achieve excellence through their own actions, choices, and decisions.

# Chapter 6 – Model of Excellence

## Are All Students Leaders?

E$\frac{L}{A}$ As some readers are already wondering by now, "Is she stating that all students will or can become leaders?" Making no such claim, only a suggestion that some individuals may decide that they do not wish to have the leader responsibilities, or they may even view a leader position as an unwelcome burden. This is an equally important learning experience for students. Regardless of whether or not a student makes a conscious choice to take on a leadership position, the process of the learning experience has not been lost. This student has experienced an opportunity to learn the dynamics of effective performance, interpersonal interactions, and leader characteristics. Development of leadership skills for this type of individual is to equip him/her with the tools needed to be successful. Success realization occurs when a situation arises and no leader is present, but this student takes action using the learned tools.

Some individuals may chose to remain actively involved and have a positive influence on the environment through positions not necessarily having the same level or type of responsibility required of a leader. An individual of this type probably chooses to stay in the background. However, he/she continues to provide services as an active member of the team. This student actively participates and makes quality contributions within any organization as it moves forward and accomplishes its stated goals and objectives. Taking on a leadership role, regardless of training, cannot be forcefully required. Others may even make statements about how successful the student would be as a leader, but once stated that he/she has no intentions of serving as a leader, or holding a leadership position, don't push the issue any further. Great care to avoid perceptions by the student or others as this student having a diminished level of self-worth or contributions because of his/her choice is the responsibility of the leadership development personnel.

For too long, being on the receiving end of an education has had the perception by many students as a mechanism that is frustrating and a detriment to their self-worth causing both psychological and physical harm (Kanungo & Mendonca, 1996). Abraham Maslow, humanistic psychologist, stated the following (as cited in Schultz, 2001), "the full use and exploitation of talents, capacities, potentialities, etc. Such people seem to be fulfilling themselves and to be doing the best that they are capable of doing. They are people who have developed or are developing the full stature of which they are capable." C. H. Patterson (as cited in Schultz, 2001), used the research of both Abraham Maslow and Carl Rogers, and he identified defining characteristics one of which is the process of self-actualization. He stated that self-actualization leads to greater self-confidence and self-efficacy.

## Principles of Leadership Course

Along with serving as the C. E. Ellison High School Leadership Academy Coordinator came the responsibility of teaching the *Principles of Leadership* course to members. Two years prior, seven advisors had developed the program's curriculum using a modular format. In the course of advisor resignations and a lack of showing or commitment to the program, some of the modules were lost and those found were incomplete. Using a combination of leadership books and resources, the first semester's curriculum using all of the following: *The 7 Habits of Highly Effective People* (Covey, 1989), *Who Moved My Cheese? An Amazing Way to Deal with Change in Your Work and in Your Life* (Johnson, 1998), and *The Leader's Companion: Insights on Leadership Through the Ages* (Wren, 1995). The first semester of the *Principles of Leadership* course is as an elective credit. During the second semester, I developed curriculum using the textbook from the college course entitled, *Leadership: Theory, Application, Skill development* (Lussier& Achua, 2004). This textbook provided students with real world examples, skill development, and insight about the dynamics of leadership. Members received Pre-AP speech credit for the second semester of the course.

Student leadership training focused on equipping students with the knowledge and skills needed to identify leadership characteristics, theories, and applications. Prominent leaders such as Gandhi, Martin Luther King, Hilary Clinton, and others became topics for in depth discussions. Students were encouraged to start trying to identify the components of their own leadership styles. In addition to encouragement, students decided on the "best fit" leadership style that allowed them to comfortably and effectively accomplish their stated goals and objectives. This was a task accomplished by providing students small-scale internal tasks and assignments. Implementation of this portion of the course helped students to identify their own strengths and weaknesses. The result of redesigning the curriculum was a magnification of the student's strengths. The student's weaker areas of growth were either further developed, or left to other students who showed strength in that particular area. In groups, students practiced what they learned during the semester, and identified real-world needs of their internal community. Small groups of students completed and presented assignments while providing possible solutions for the identified areas of need to the entire class in proposal format. The speech requirement for the course was satisfied during this portion of the redesigned curriculum.

*Leadership in Action* was a new concept that I had added to the program. In this portion of training, students were required to plan, propose, develop, and implement a project that would have a positive impact on their internal (school) or external (surrounding community) environments. I served as a presenter at two different conferences, and I saw these invitations as an opportunity to receive feed back about the *Leadership in Action* inclusion to the program. I took some of my students to the conferences with me so that they could present their projects and experiences. On February 17, 2004, eight students presented their projects at the 2004 National Association of African American Studies where they received positive comments and feedback from the conference attendees about their project presentations. During the Texas Association for the Gifted and Talented (TAGT) Leadership Conference on April 16, 2004, a different group of six students presented their projects and again received positive feedback, comments, and business cards from interested conference attendees immediately following their presentations. The students provided the conference attendees with details of their selected projects, vision statement and mission statements along with their project's progress at the point of the conference date. Conference attendees were amazed that such young students believed they were capable of changing their environments and they were taking steps to make their belief systems become reality.

## 2004 Project Symposium

During the *Leadership in Action* phase of training a single student or a small group of students began to work on a selected internal or external community service based project. The final stage of the *Leadership in Action* training was for the students to present their community service-based projects. On April 19, 2004, the 2004 Project Symposium took place at C. E. Ellison High School. All participants (members, board of directors, community leaders, teachers, and principal) scored the senior projects based on their ability to clearly articulate the project vision and mission statements, adhere to the established project guidelines as outlined in the project guidance worksheet, and overall presentation of the community service based project. A score of 80% or higher had been established as an indicator of successful project completion and implementation.

I hold strongly to my belief that student leadership development along with a community service based project is an effective method to increase a student's level of self-efficacy, self-regulation, and intrinsic motivation. The community service based project allows students to actively utilize the leadership skills that they have learned. As a result, I extended community service based projects to the sophomore and junior members. Invaluable learning experiences resulted from students completing community service based projects. I do not believe that the benefits of such an experience should be a unique one available to *seniors only*, which had been the past tradition. Consequently, a student's senior year is full of deadlines, applications, and other situations that all signal that new future beginnings are fast approaching. I viewed project extension to the lower grade levels as a method that ensured that all members would have the opportunity to complete a project. Project completion by some of the seniors had been a real problem in the program's past. Additionally, completing projects in the lower grade levels removed some of the stress of student's senior if it became too overwhelming. These younger students would have already reaped the rewards and benefits of the project experience.

Community service-based projects builds student awareness and allows him/her to experience the powerful effects of influencing their environment in a real world setting. Knowledge, processes, and confidence that community service based project bestowed upon students was transferred to other areas within the students lives such as academics, scholarship applications, community service, employment, and many others. The result of the entire project experience built student self-awareness, awareness of inner strength, power, and intrinsic motivation all having positive influences in the student's daily living. Students began to view their ability of striving to achieve academic excellence simply as a means of getting through the next preparatory steps of life that would enable them to ultimately accomplish their future goals. I saw no reason to reserve these opportunities for growth and experiences until a student had reached his/her senior year. I also envisioned the community service based project experience during the earlier high school years as a means to assist the younger students in the identification of areas that need enhancing with more practice.

Sophomore and junior members that presented in 2004 would undergo the same scoring system in 2005 and 2006, as did the senior members in 2004. As seniors, these students could choose to use their completed project for the 2004 Project Symposium, or complete an additional project. The student's selected choice of the project would be the one that they considered to best reflect their overall abilities as a leader. I suspect that many of students will choose the latter option since some students have already been asking about completing additional projects for next year. Some of the sophomore and junior members have stated that they would like to serve as mentors for the new 2004-2005 members and assist them as they complete their projects.

## Answering Specific Questions

In addition to the course's curriculum redesign, *Leadership in Action*, community service based project, and real world experiences, I also wanted to provide answers to specific questions that I had. I needed a method to calculate and collect data about the use of community service based projects as an effective method to increase a student's level of self-efficacy, self-regulation, and intrinsic motivation I wanted to develop answers for the following questions:

1. Could the project experience serve as a guide to students as they approached new situations?
2. What would be the long-term effects of the community service based project experience?
3. Is there a relationship between the community service based project experience and student academic achievement?
4. Is there a link between the community service based project experience and the student's ability to strive for excellence in various environments?

Answers to these questions are located at the end of this section, but a partial answer resulted from the 2004 Project Symposium Presentations that follow:

1. The Cultural Exchange coordinated by a senior member
2. Ellison High School Marquee Project coordinated by two senior members
3. 2004 B.A.E.H. Youth Leadership Conference and B.A.E.H. Scholarship Fund established by two senior members
4. Leaders of the Past and their influences coordinated by a senior member
5. Revolution coordinated by a junior member
6. David Lubar Author's Visit coordinated by a sophomore and junior member
7. Heart of Texas Discovery coordinated by a sophomore member
8. Building Blocks to the Future coordinated by a junior member
9. Leading Throughout the Nation coordinated by a sophomore member
10. History of the C. E. Ellison High School Leadership Academy coordinated by a sophomore member
11. Lenna Black's Ambassador Experience coordinated by a junior member
12. Student Responsibility & Accountability coordinated by a sophomore member
13. The Emerald's Little Gems established by a junior member
14. Ellison High School versus Temple High School Blood Drive coordinated by three junior members with Scott and White Hospital
15. Public Relations coordinated by a junior member
16. The Eagle Eyes On the Future coordinated by a sophomore member

## Leadership Defined

Centuries of research on the topic of defining leadership, philosophical discussions, and seemingly endless investigations have taken place in search of discovering an encompassing definition of leadership. Kouzes and Posner (1997) define leadership as the ability to mobilize a group of people towards the accomplishment of a common set of goals. On January 31, 2004 at the 2004 B.A.E.H. (Brandon Antal and Edward Huncherick, 2004) Youth Leadership Conference in

Killeen, Texas, Dr. Ann Farris, KISD Deputy Superintendent, used the phrase "leadership is a verb". This phrase used by Dr. Farris directly relates to my own definition of leadership. I believe that leadership is more than abilities, characteristics, or skills. To offer a clear understanding of my definition of leadership, I will address four major components in the definition separately.

1. *Leadership is a process.* This portion of the definition indicates that leadership or students developing into effective leaders will not be something that occurs overnight. As students learn about the various leadership theories, skills, and begin their own development into leaders, they also learn and become equipped to identify their areas of strengths and weaknesses. These students are then able to try, test, and refine their behaviors to accommodate this new knowledge.

2. *Developing the power to visualize future environments.* One of the most important tasks of an effective leader is having an ability to anticipate changes that are occurring resultant of societal and national expectations, needs, and/or global interactions. Developing the ability to foresee future environments is where a leader gets the power and drive for his/her passion toward the achievement of specific goals.

3. In order for student leaders to *develop a willingness to take part in planning, individual growth, and implementing necessary resources* they must believe that it is okay "dream big dreams". They need to have opportunities to uncover the difference between simply dreaming, setting realistic goals, and becoming actively involved to accomplish their stated goals.

4. The last portion of the definition, *to make the vision become reality* is the end-result or product of all of the actions taken by these students as they relate their actions as a necessary portion of leadership development.

Now take in the definition as a whole so that it accurately depicts my students as they take on their roles as effective leaders of the future. *Leadership is the process of developing the power to visualize future environments, a willingness to take part in planning, individual growth, and implementing necessary resources to make visions become reality.* Does this definition provide a visual image that epitomizes a leader? The visual image for me is a belief in our future leaders (high school students) of society actively seeking methods and the means to effectively change their environments and leaving an imprint in the hearts and minds of a greater society because of their actions. High school students, very similar to my students, receiving the proper guidance, support, experiences, and opportunities promoted by the passion of their leaders can learn to achieve the same goals as stated in this definition of leadership. One way for other high school students to achieve at this same level is through the components of the *Model of Excellence* that I developed and implemented.

## Model of Excellence

## Student Leadership Development

Early theorists suggested that individuals are born as leaders, but Hackman & Johnson (1995) stated, "Leaders are made, not born". Smith (1995) suggested that leadership skill development could be taught in the public school system. Smith's suggesting supports the idea of the African proverb, "it takes a village to raise a child." Educators can have a lasting impression or impact on an individual's leadership development. Covey (1989) suggested that if the goal is to train an individual to accomplish something, then the goals of training used should "Begin with the end in mind". To obtain the desired results, students need guided training and practice giving direction to their goals. In order to develop as leaders, individuals will need opportunities to lead (Gardner, 1990). Conditioning for the desirable characteristics of leadership development begins in the home, and further enhancement could occur within the school system (Covey, 1989). The real evidence of leadership becomes apparent because of the lifelong decisions that an individual chooses (Maxwell, 1999). An individual is equipped to make better life-sustaining choices when his/her emotional resources are utilized (Payne, 1998).

One is able to infer that individuals will not become leaders overnight by the use of the word *development.* In other words, the individual undergoing leadership role transitions, should not expect to find immediate evidence of its existence (Smith, 1995). By definition, development means to make active and promote growth (Merriam-Webster's Collegiate Dictionary, 1998). My use of the term development means the active promotion of academic inquiry through engaging experiences that result in student achievement and growth into life-long learners. When students obtain development in this sense, the bar of standards and academic achievement automatically raises. How is that some may ask? These students are able to comprehend the "sum of the parts making up the whole". Students undergoing leadership training exhibit a renewed perception of their position and responsibilities in a democratic society.

## Community Service-Based Projects

According to Miller (2002), both the internal and external mechanisms of memory development influence an individual's capacity to learn. He also stated, "reliable memory is developed as a result of a child deciding what works best, recall, and reflections about the habits of the learning process and teaching the child a concept of strategy does not ensure that it will be transferred to another task". Miller's statement can explain some of the reasons that standardized testing results most often do not equate to what the student actually has learned or knows. I attribute the interest level of an individual from one task to another as an underlying factor in his/her ability to transfer learning into new or different environments. When the level of interest is low, the individual lacks the ability to personalize a need to actively participate in the experience of learning. What the student has learned in one particular content area remains confined to that class and as the student continues the day's activities no opportunities to connect what was learned earlier takes place. I believe that exposing students to, and allowing them to dig deeper into their areas of interest enhances their ability to find a real and personal need to learn about new topics or subjects that they originally perceived as having little to no real value. Actions and statements made by my students affirm my belief.

## Self-Directed Learners

*Self-efficacy* defined as the individual's perceived capacity to execute a behavior required for a desired outcome and can affect motivation and behavior (Roth, 1985). Failed efforts to achieve desired outcomes due to conscious or subconscious individual delay, procrastination, has been stated as a reduced focus on the future (Jackson, Fritch, Nagasaka, & Pope, 2003). According to Bandura (as cited in Miller, 2002), parents and teachers can enhance children's self-efficacy by drawing attention to the positive aspects of their performance that causes a repeat of the behavior. A high degree of self-efficacy will in turn elevate the individual's ability to use his/her self-regulating behaviors that will allow the realization and achievement of high academic standards. The public education system can effectively accomplish the goal of promoting academic excellence through the development of programs that heighten student's knowledge of self. Individuals will approach difficult tasks from a unique perspective. More importantly, individuals having self-awareness (self-efficacy) will know when to seek the assistance, and effectively accomplish a task.

*Self-regulation* is the combination of internal thought processes and external actions that an individual undergoes toward the accomplishment of a goal. Recent research findings have suggested that an individual's inability to self-regulate his/her behavior results in failed goal attainment. Individual perceptions of experiences and the individual's inability to plan for future goal achievement causes reduced motivation (Jackson, Fritch, Nagasaka, & Pope, 2003). According to Schunk (2001), having the ability to self-regulate in order to accomplish a goal is an important concept in an individual's development and the individual's ability to remain focused and committed to lifelong learning. As stated by Martinez-Pons (2002), much of this learning must be self-initiated and self-directed. Engaging individuals in self-reflection will enhance the ability to identify his/her strengths and weaknesses as related to attaining higher levels of academic success. Reflection will also allow individuals to modify their behavior and embrace desired goals. Having opportunities to practice and refine the skills of self-regulation will lead an individual to experience an elevation in his/her levels of self-efficacy.

*Intrinsic motivation* is the force that drives an individual's action, and specific behavior exhibited to accomplish a goal that essentially becomes internalized (Merriam-Webster's Collegiate Dictionary, 1998). Educational credit cites intrinsic motivation as having positive results on task completion and satisfaction, promote growth, and satisfy higher order needs (Patrick, Hisley, Kempler, & College, 2000). Miller (2002) stated that a child's level of motivation is determined through learning by observing. The child performs a task after observing the specific behavior performed by an adult, and repeats the behavior based on elevated parental or adult approval rating for three types of reinforcements called motives: past, promised, and vicarious (Boeree, 2003; Koslowski & Condry, 1977). Variables that affect motivation can be a consequence of societal change, parental support, and encouragement (Canter & Canter, 2001).

I believe that the combined development of self-efficacy, self-regulation, and intrinsic motivation are the precursors for student development into self-directed learners. As self-directed learners, students are more apt to investigate new topics, situations, or environments simply for the sake of increasing their knowledge base. Curiosity becomes an asset rather than something that causes an individual to get off the course of their goal. These of type learners invite new information or challenges as a method to keep their problem-solving skills lubricated. **CAUTION STATEMENT**: To the self-directed learner: Utilize your skills with care.

One problem seems to consistently arise in the life of the self-directed learner. Individuals not possessing this same driving force or ambition will often view the self-directed learner as a "know it all" and this view may lead to hostile interactions or feelings. A problem that presents itself is not necessarily one that is waiting or even wanting its solution or discovery to come from the self-directed learner. Take care and allow others to take part in the game of solving problems. Sometimes the self-directed learner is oblivious to the type of negative perceptions that may exist because he/she thinks that everyone has and utilizes the same system or skills to solve problems. This is a misconception and is definitely a big NO, NO.

## Academic Accountability

Ultimately, successful experiences generate students who are capable of becoming committed to lifelong learning. As stated by Martinez-Pons (2002), much of this learning must be self-initiated and self-directed. As students committed to lifelong learning they also recognize these learned skills and place them into their mental toolbox of success. Students can then easily transfer these developed skills into other environments. The ability to accomplish specific goals or to become risk takers in novice situations due to these developed skills will provide them with greater future endeavor ratios of success. According to Murray (2000), students will also need to strategically develop a plan to achieve their academic goals that include the time to reflect on their selected learning technique.

A raised bar for higher academic performance, expectations, and standards for all students becomes a realistic possibility when students develop these skills. Additionally, students strive to achieve their best and are capable of accomplishing their stated goals. The processes utilized by an individual that result in success, or aids the individual in arriving at an intended goal, needs to be calibrated for future uses. Opportunities to use processes that have resulted in success need repeating in both formal and informal settings. This assures the student that his/her success did not simply occur by chance. After successful completion of a task, time to reflect on the event allows the student to identify many positive and negative aspects of the process. In this fashion, the student learns to fully recognize his/her skills and becomes a part of the student's repertoire for solving problems or taking action on a daily basis in varying environments.

Using the components of the ME and FIP-2004 with the members of the C. E. Ellison High School Leadership Academy has proven to assist students develop and connect this awareness. Students know and believe that they should always strive to achieve their best regardless of the environment (academic, extracurricular activity, or employment). During interviews with the current members of the 2004-2005 school year, several of the students gave examples about how they had experienced changes in their original perceptions. The perceptual changes for these students related mostly to the need for them to achieve their academic best. Some stated that their change in perception resulted from training that they received during the 2003-2004 school year.

Some students stated that they began to take more challenging courses such as, Advanced Placement and Pre-AP courses. They said that this had resulted from their desire to excel in a rigorous academic program. Some also stated that they were able to achieve at higher academic levels because of the performance of their peers and teacher expectations. C. E. Ellison High School has benefited from the leadership development of these students because they have the ability to transfer what they have learned into other environments. For example, C. E. Ellison High School Leadership Academy members hold the top leadership positions in Student Council, National Honor Society, Band, International Club, and many others. Another example occurred soon after the Texas Assessment of Knowledge and Skills (TAKS) writing test. Several students came back from the test and stated that the writing portion of the test was easy because of discussions, writing about real world topics, and learning about the dynamics of interpersonal relationship in the Principles of Leadership class. These students have experienced a change in perception about their personal accountability for their individual academic performance.

Just imagine entire public schools in different communities, states, and throughout a nation filled with students having this much insight. Even still, imagine the manner in which these students will approach goals they want in the future. Think about how dynamic and powerful students with this much insight would be taking the lead in our nation. Think about these students as adults taking on future roles in a democratic society. Imagine the quality of learning that is passed down to future generations with these types of adults making decisions about the nation's future goals, global standing by other nations, and as parents. Just imagine.

The mindset of most programs designed for leadership training today, are for adult or post-secondary individuals. *Process* is a word commonly used to describe an individual's path into leadership development. Use of the term *process* indicates that leadership development will not occur overnight. There is a need for programs whose aim is the goal of developing leaders of the future to begin preparing the individual before he/she has entered into adulthood. The methods that I utilized with the members of the C. E. Ellison High School Leadership Academy serves as an example of how an effective high school leadership development program can operate within the public school system. These students are able to carry their learned experiences with them as they enter into post-secondary education or different areas of study. What better way to train future leaders and productive citizenship than to allow students to experience concepts from a primary viewpoint?

In the following section, I address the questions that guided my development of the *Model of Excellence.*

1.  Can high school students develop the skills of an effective leader?
    a.  The answer to this question is yes, as long teacher/coordinator meets specific conditions (as outlined in the Training the Trainer section).
    b.  Charge the teacher/coordinator with the responsibility of providing leadership development instruction and opportunities for students as they develop into effective leaders.
    c.  The teacher/coordinator must buy in to the ultimate goals of high school student leadership development as I have proposed.
    d.  The teacher/coordinator must receive proper training and opportunities to experience a paradigm shift regarding high school student's ability to effectively serve as society's future leaders.
2.  Can a definition of leadership describe what high school students can do resulting from an effective leadership development model? Yes. Take another look at the leadership definition just provided.
    a.  Leadership is the process of developing the power to visualize future environments, a willingness to take part in planning, individual growth, and implementing necessary resources to make visions become reality.
3.  Will students become self-directed learners when empowered experiencing increased levels of self-efficacy, self-regulation, and intrinsic motivation through community service-based projects and outcome-based leadership development?
    a.  Yes.
    b.  Students undergoing the type of leadership development training that I advocate become aware of the expectations for doing their best that has been placed upon them.
    c.  Personal involvement and contributing to their internal and external communities through community service based project accounts for increased levels of a student's self-efficacy, self-regulation, and intrinsic motivation.
    d.  Students learn to recognize their own leadership development style and make adjustments according to a multitude of perceptions.
4.  Will leadership development and community service-based projects stimulate high school students to transfer their learning and achieving an academic best?

a. Students approach new or different environments utilizing the skills that gave them assistance as they achieved the goals in previous experiences.

b. Students learn how to quantify specific results based on predetermined measures for actions taken toward goal attainment.

c. Students determine levels of success for other areas of their daily lives.

5. What will you see to support the belief that high school students have developed into effective leaders?

a. You will see high school students operating at higher cognitive levels in multiple settings.

b. High school students completing community service based projects that would prove to be a task for the average actively involved post-secondary student or adult resulting in success.

c. High school students willing to remain actively involved in influencing their environments.

## Model of Excellence: The Eight Phases

The goals of ME are ones of developing responsible and accountable students with the reward of education ownership and to provide research evidence that supports the claims being made. The following sections include the eight-phase outline of the ME that I developed and used to achieve successful student leadership development during my research. Audiences composed of educational practitioners, policy makers, parents and those having interests in the success of public education can all benefit from these research, findings, and examples. Successful use of the eight phases listed here assumes that the program coordinator and other personnel responsible for the successful implementation of student leadership development have received effective leadership development training (suggestions are included in a later chapter).

## Phase 1: Modeling

In addition to the information addressed in the Student Leadership Development section, the primary textbook of instruction is the *Leadership: Theory, Application, Skill development* (Lussier& Achua, 2004). The other books aid students as they identify their personal leadership styles, become aware of leadership terminology, and experience leadership paradigm shifts. Students learn to identify the characteristics, theories, skills, and their own leadership style, strengths, and weaknesses. While still in phase I, students also complete multiple internal and external environmental group assignments to become familiar with the meaning and implementation of the community service-based project criteria (vision, mission, goals, reflection, internal and external environments, action, and environmental impact). These activities serve as a representation of small successes of a student's ability to make a positive difference in their immediate environment.

## Phase II: Active Planning

While continuing the Modeling phase, the second phase, begins. During the phase II, students have opportunities to brainstorm possible projects that may serve as a method for them to effectively influence their environment. At this point, students may want to identify their partners based on shared or similar interest for a particular topic. Students must be allowed class time to discuss and plan their projects in small groups (each member completes a community service-based project planning contract) or as single student groups. At this point, the training coordinator can begin teaching the students how to develop simple surveys to that will help determine the benefits or contributions that a particular project may provide. The use of surveys is also an effective method of gaining knowledge about areas within the school that need improvement. The use of surveys may assist students in narrowing the scope of possible real- world topics for a project. The training coordinator guides all students through the phases of collecting and organizing data, computer assistance programs for data input and storage, interpreting and analyzing data, and creating visual representations of data.

## Phase III: Project Vision and Mission Statement Development

During phase III, students begin to develop rough-drafts of their project vision and mission statements (refined as students investigate and plan to utilize specific elements and resources for the implementation of their projects). During the latter portion of phase III, students receive both the *Community Service-Based Project Criteria* and the *Project Guidance Worksheet.* The training coordinator must explain to the students that each community service-based project must include all of the criteria listed on these forms. Another component explained at this point is that each student or group of students will receive a project grade during the Project Symposium Presentation based on his/her ability to incorporate each of the listed criteria. The *Community Service-Based Project Criteria* and *Project Guidance Worksheet* is an effective method of ensuring that all students begin with the same advantages for success and that they receive full credit for all aspects of their projects, and it also maximizes overall percentages for the students.

## Phase IV: Present Project Proposals

During phase IV, students refine their project mission and vision statements for a final product. The training coordinator asks questions about specific project characteristics to ensure that the students have covered a variety of possible problems or situations that may arise during the project implementation phase. Once the problem-solving and critical thinking phase is completed, the training coordinator starts teaching the students how to write a formal project proposal. The formal project proposal will then be transferred into a PowerPoint® presentation for the educational stakeholders.

After students have presented their proposal presentations to the educational stakeholders, they will undergo a question and answer session. Educational stakeholders, defined as anyone having an interest in the success of public education, (school board members, members of the Board of Directors [if one has been established], booster club members, district personnel, community/business leaders, family members, teachers to include student's coaches, media, and friends) individuals are all encouraged to ask questions specific to projects. The question and answer sessions ensure a wide variety of differing perceptions and perspectives are considered. Once the recording of all participant votes is completed, the student receives formal permission to continue with his/her project. *Permission granted occurs under the provisions of real-world learning experience, ability to positively influence the internal or external environments, and financial costs.* The participant interaction portion of the project proposal presentations serves to develop the student's sense of membership and belonging, ability to encourage others, ability to learn from mistakes made, stimulate student levels of self-efficacy, leadership growth and development, and intrinsic motivation.

## Phase V: Project Advertising

During phase V, the training coordinator teaches the students how to create brochures, posters (hand created and computer generated), develop formal letters, formal participant invitations, and methods of contacting the media (local newspaper, radio stations, and local television stations) to advertise their community service-based projects. All student developed documents, forms, and interview simulations must occur before students contact members of the community, community leaders, or for business leader interactions.

## Phase VI: Leadership in Action

During phase VI, students meet in class to hear program updates or community service opportunities. The training coordinator now takes on the role of a facilitator. Students are already familiar with behavior expectations, time management skills needed, ability to self-regulate, and their ability to accomplish their stated goals. Students work independently as they complete the final preparations for their community service-based projects. The training coordinator ensures the even distribution of project tasks by reviewing the community service-based project planning contracts. At this point, the training coordinator only offers suggestions and assistance as the students finalize and fine-tune the preparations for completing their projects. Students develop surveys or questionnaires about specific

48

aspects of their projects. They will use this information for data input analysis into visual interpretation portion of their project presentations. Students complete their projects on Saturdays or during a school day if the project includes the internal environment. Students coordinate their projects with Student Activities and ensure that facilities and dates are conflict free.

## Phase VII: Project Symposium

During phase VII, students consolidate all of their data, pictures taken during project implementation, and send invitations to all stakeholders (school board members, members of the Board of Directors [if one has been established, booster club members], district personnel, community/business leaders, family members, teachers to include student's coaches, media, and friends) to attend Project Symposium Presentations. After each presentation, there is a question and answer session. Once students have completed and presented their projects, they become project mentors for other students working on the final stages of their projects. The training coordinator still acting as facilitator, now has project assistants who serve as role models for the other students. This portion of the program increases the project assistant's (participating student's) level of self-efficacy, self-regulation, and intrinsic motivation to learn and share their learning with other students.

## Phase VIII: Sharing the Project Experience

During phase VIII, students store their project presentations on compact disk to serve as an example for the following year's members. Students also complete a cover letter, resume, and electronic portfolio to serve as evidence of the student's accomplishments while participating in the training. Additionally, the training coordinator actively seeks opportunities that allow students to show case their projects and learning experiences at local, state and national levels. As mentioned earlier, my students presented their projects at the National Association of African American Studies (NAAAS) in Houston, Texas and at the Texas Association for the Gifted and Talented (TAGT) Leadership Conference in Austin, Texas.

## Student Leadership Development Research Continues

I continue to conduct high school student development research because as I first began my search for methods to measure the degree of accomplishing certain goals and objectives, I found an absence in measurement components in many of the guidelines and standards that are being supported by government and state agencies. The absence of measurable components existed in the identification of students gifted and talented in leadership. In addition to this absence, as far as high school student leadership development was concerned many programs that exist in public schools that have the support of national organizations claiming leadership as a focus, does not usually go beyond the use of the word leadership.

I started to ask myself, "What type of leaders are the sponsors involved these programs?" Not meaning to imply that these individual's leadership goals and training were completely of no benefit to students, it just became evident to me that these individuals had received no formal leadership training. While interviewing new prospective students for the C. E. Ellison High School Leadership Academy Program, many of which were members in some of the school clubs to which I just referred, I asked the question, "What does leadership mean to you?" There were a variety of answers, but many of the students held a leader perception as someone holding a position and telling others what to do. This is not my picture of a leader, as I would guess it is not the picture held in the minds of most individuals. Not in today's successful organizations at least.

It is my belief that it is not enough simply to provide information, lay down the ground rules, or give permission for specific programs and think that the mission has been accomplished. To state *"mission accomplished"* at that point is grossly premature. This is my view about some of the programs promoted by both state and national leaders whose positions allow them the rights and freedoms to do so. More times than not, evidence that there has been a lack of planning and troubleshooting for state and national programs shows its true face in time. In addition to these lacking areas, there exists the appearance that no or at least little real thought processes were put into effect beyond the immediate demand that public school systems implement the new programs. In cases such as this, the overall result of having implemented the program towards the goals and objectives of providing long-term results is an oversight.

As a result, the current process continues which is to draft information about and for the new program, mass produce, and disseminate the incomplete information to the various district and/or states. All of this has taken place without providing any information that leads to assessing if the standards and guidelines have been achieved. I believe this to be true, even when the existence and reasoning for the program has been explained and explained again in an attempt to offer the impression of program clarity. I have noticed a multitude of government and state documents in which the wording begins to have the same tone, the only difference is that it has new title attached. When state and national leaders grant permission to hold public school systems accountable for achieving the goals and objectives of particular programs or requirements, with the intent of student achievement and success, it must also be the responsibility of these same leaders to provide educational stakeholders with a complete set of measurement mechanisms.

Without a system in place that will ask the difficult questions of measurement, need to see real evidence of program intervention, the real world potential of reaching the overall majority of students attending the public school systems, then we as a nation are still continuing to just spin our wheels going nowhere. Without a real method of gauging whether or not a program has met, exceeded, or show progress towards achievement of clear and concise guidelines and standards; the program might as well not exist. Any action by state or national leaders that falls short of ensuring that an effective measurement system is in place before a program is implemented, assures one thing; program failure. These individual's actions have also ensured that those individuals who eagerly "bad mouth" the public school system's ability to educate have their needed ammunition ready to fire at anyone who defends the public school system.

Remember what I stated earlier, identifying the problem is one of the simplest acts or responsibilities that an individual can have. Listen to the words of my brother Adrian who stated, "If you can't or won't be a part of the *solution*, then *you* are part of the problem." The state's guarantee to educate its people took place long ago. Yet how quickly some have already forgotten that famous report in 1983 that caused so many to wake up, *A Nation at Risk* (National Commission on Excellence in Education, 1983). I believe that problems in education today are due partly to lack of accountability for those having the authority to design and implement programs carelessly or rather incompletely.

I find it somewhat ironic that two of the areas I focus on for student leadership development in the Model of Excellence is student responsibility and accountability. It seems that state and national leaders are not responsible or accountable for their own actions, imagine the advantage start that my former students will have over this type of leader. Just imagine it.

# Chapter 7 – Student Transformation

**Long-Term Goals**

ELA. The strict adherence to a standard set of guidelines allowed us to remain safe and continue to live as a family. We relied heavily on one another to remain strong and to "do the right things" in even in the absence of parental guidance. We were always aware of the importance of effectively accomplishing this task. Our mother candidly explained to us the real life consequences for our family's ability to remain united if we failed to follow her rules and guidelines. The public education system should work much in the same way. Educational decisions about the inclusion of specific programs or training for students in the public education system needs to based on what I call the *four long-term standards of student transformation*.

First, students must know *why it is important* for them to establish high standards of excellence for their futures. This is best shown to students by providing them with opportunities to interact with community leaders and professionals employed in the student's identified area of interest through internships or mentor programs. Second, students must understand the *real world* consequences that lay ahead if they fail to be receptive of a quality education. Again, delegation of this task should go the local community leaders for fulfillment of this standard. Components of local community leader delegation for this standard needs to include candid information; whether it be positive or negative and shared with students. The *real world* design of student transformation allows students to reflect on their current actions toward accomplishing their dreams. Additionally, it also to ensures that the students have a designed plan of to overcome established habits that could inhibit them from fully realizing their dreams. Third, students must understand the important need for them to be *receptive to a quality education*. This standard is enhanced through employment and tradeshow fairs where personnel holding top positions from specific organizations or businesses share their list of citizenship characteristics, education quality, and levels of training that they seek when considering individuals for employment and/or services.

Finally, students must learn and act in manners that depict their *value and appreciation for differences between individuals*, how differences can offer an array of new contributions to the group as a whole. True appreciation of differences and values between individuals means a mutual sharing and understanding of an individual's belief origins, ideas, and cultures. Without this standard clearly in place, global divisions that are currently apparent in this nation and globally will continue. Appreciation and value divisions are often the result of an individual's perception that he/she is not fully appreciated or valued due to individual differences of opinions, life-style choices, and many others. Valuing and appreciating differences does not mean that individuals give up who they are to accommodate a uniform likeness or appearance there of. It means simply that individuals are working to gain insight about the underlying thoughts behind the specific actions or beliefs of others. This standard allows students to experience changes in their original perceptions about the worth of individuals who are different. At the same time, valuing and appreciating differences does not mean the exclusion of any population or culture that is involved. In this country, too many times these words have been misunderstood or misinterpreted to mean valuing and appreciating differences based on minority cultures. Some individuals have used this misinterpreted meaning of valuing and appreciating differences, failing to realize as the word minority implies that there is also a majority. Too many times, in America this has meant that the overlooked focus of uniting all people as one occurs causing cultures to constantly be at odds with each other in the attempt to validate their own culture. Exclusion of any individual or any people serves only to heighten the intensity and cause resentment toward the value and appreciation of different cultures, and add more torque to cultural relations that are already strained.

Use of the phrase, "valuing and appreciating the differences of others", is an inclusion of all cultures. Having this type of perception of others is the manner in which valuable lessons are learned. I stand for the development of intercultural relationships where a variety of cultures are working hand in hand for the common good of all humans always keeping the global perspective in clear view. The *four long-term standards of student transformation* will influence the manner in which students will approach their dreams and decision-making processes in the future. Students are able to infer end results and the magnitude of their position or actions in the future if they fail to accomplish even one of the *four long-term standards of student transformation*. Student leadership development is the effective method to ensure that students have the opportunity to accomplish the *four long-term standards of student transformation* to the fullest capacity and availability within environmental specifics.

## Stimulating the "Want to Learn" Mentality

When an individual wants something bad enough, he/she will become a problem-solver, use available resources, and become creatively motivated to take action to remove obstacles in order to accomplish the goal. Key here is the word *want*. Establishing goals and expectations for student achievement in the public education system must include the implementation of programs that allows students to develop a *"want to learn"* mentality. In order for this to occur, educational leaders and policy makers will have to experience a paradigm shift about a student's ability to achieve the goal of educational ownership. Some students already possess an internal driving force that allows them to *"want to learn"* new concepts and ideas. It is safe to say that in the grand scheme of things in the public school system; a total number of students that behave in this manner are of a minority population. What happens then with the majority of students attending public schools? Well, some students fall into the minimal pass category, others become bored or frustrated and drop out of school, some students attend school because it is the law until they reach a certain age, while still others cram and purge information for the purpose of doing well on exams or assignments to maintain high GPA's. This last category of students mentioned performs well on exams or assignments, but one or two weeks later, these students view the same material as something that is unfamiliar. Students need to have experiences based on their area of interest to truly develop a *"want to learn"* mentality. They will have the ability to establish realistic and attainable goals once this mentality becomes worthwhile to them as they visualize their futures.

One way that this is successfully accomplished is through a mentor program. Once a student has learned the specific skills needed for a particular area of interest through conversations, activities, and experimentation in a protégé environment his/her desire to learn increasingly internalizes. Student, often used in this research because of the focus of this research, but this same idea exists for adults as well based on a *want or desire to learn* something. Next, comes the motivating factor that provides the individual with the drive to take action. Sometimes experiences that give drive to accomplish the *want or desire to learn* are not positive. Matter of fact the driving force behind a variety of innovative inventions or accomplishments arose from negative experiences or even an individual's natural need to compete. A skilled or resourceful individual has the ability to use negative experiences to drive positive outcomes. Development of this skill is a need in the lives and daily routines of both students and adults.

## Reality Check

Students will often base their future goals or aspirations for a particular profession on how a television show depicts it, or on the glamour that they associate with its title. Countless times I have asked students about their goals for the future to only receive an unrealistic answer or idea. Sometimes the response was realistic based on the student's level of motivation, interest to investigate further, or access to information or technology at home. However, more often than not, a student simply gave a quick and unrealistic response. For example, a student may state that he/she wants to attend college to become a doctor. Yet, he/she either avoids or despises the rigorous instruction and activities in courses such as, advanced placement chemistry, biology, or calculus. In this example, the student's future goal was not a realistic one. Providing students with the opportunity to observe, interact, and participate in specific activities with individuals already holding positions in their professed area of interest (mentors) allows misconception corrections and opportunities to reflect upon and try to establish realistic goals. This paints a better picture of reality for the students before paying for classes in college in which the student later finds they had no real interest or desire to take in the first place. With today's cost of post-secondary education, this can be a costly lesson for both the student and his/her family.

A picture of reality through a mentor program while still in high school provides a student with two different actions. One action would be for this new found reality to cause the student to make a concerted effort to develop a solid academic foundation, utilize a systematic method of self-discipline, self-improvement, and increase the level of motivation needed to accomplish his/her goal. A realization that there is an absence of passion or commitment for a stated professional goal would direct the next action of the student. The student still has time while in high school to investigate other professions through the mentoring program. Providing students with the opportunity to realistically explore a particular profession, or the removal of the unrealistic glamour associated with a profession of interest before they enter into a post-secondary program, provides invaluable information and experiences for these students.

The experience also provides the student with the tools necessary to make informed decisions about whether or not he/she should pursue a particular profession. The final decision must be that of the student. Students who have had the experience of participating in a mentor program while still in high school has the ability of using his/her reflection skills and base the final decision on the ability to realistically accomplish the prerequisites for the profession. Students will also make assessments about a particular profession based on individual level of academic skill development, passion for, or desire to develop the identified skills. A combination of using these methods will provide students with invaluable insight for the future as participants in an effectively conducted high school mentor program.

## Mentor Program

Various business organizations, educational facilities, and others have mentoring programs. Viewed as expert in his/her field, an individual serves as a mentor to someone less skilled. The concept of utilizing the skills of the best personnel in an organization to help a new individual or less experienced (protégé) assimilate into the established culture and environment is definitely an idea geared towards effective organizations. Mrs. Pat Levi served as my mentor and threw out a lifeline of support during my first year of teaching. At the time, her brother was the Curriculum Instructional Specialist, and he called her at home and explained that he had assigned her as a mentor for a new teacher. Within 15 minutes, Pat came into work specifically to meet the new teacher during her summer vacation. That was quite impressive because her actions made gave the feeling that first year teacher success was important to her.

One of the first things that she said was important to remember was, "the most important thing to remember as a first year teacher is survival". She even provided a "survival kit" that consisted of classroom rules, a safety goggle song, and many other items. Having never served as a public school teacher, this was a very important act. The difference between having a successful or unsuccessful first year of teaching depends heavily on the manner in which a new teacher conducts the first day of class. Quickly learning just how important once the "first year teacher" stories about classroom management and discipline issues circulated around the school. Pat also provided a grand tour of the entire science department and school. Later, when school had finally started, introductions to all of the science department teachers took place. Mrs. Levi also made sure that I knew where to go to get needed supplies. The importance of teacher, school, district, and state expectations for student learning emphasis is constant along with the expectations of a teacher's ability to teach. All of these teaching skills developed due to her expertise, patience, and helpful ideas.

Pat did not overwhelm her new protégé by giving endless lists of statements, requirements, and information all at one time. We had a variety of informal contact with one another where she would share bits and pieces of information. For instance, we met in her home, during lunch breaks, during conferences, and Pat would always ask how things were going, and we met each other's family members. Mrs. Levi watched my son, dropped him off at school, and picked him after school while I attended an out of town conference and my husband was attending a military school in Virginia. We developed a wonderful friendship.

Contrary to these personal and positive protégé experiences, horror stories surfaced from some of the other new teachers participating in the mentor/protégé program. In summary, some of the stories sounded like unpleasant experience. This portion of the mentor/protégé experience serves only to show the value and benefits for individual growth and success when a good mentor exists. Personal relationships develop through successful mentor/protégé programs. The individual on the other end of the experience/expertise spectrum (protégé) feels like an important member of the team. As a result, the idea of feeling fully capable and prepared to do an outstanding job in the teaching profession developed into a realistic goal. The end benefit of this type of initial new teacher feeling for students is one where the new teacher focuses on the promotion of academic success and successful experiences for students attending public schools.

## Initiating Student Mentor/Protégé Programs

As stated earlier, students who participate in high school mentoring programs provides them with a realistic view about various professions. To effectively implement a successful student mentor program within the public school system, special care needs to exist in specific areas to ensure that the experience has been both a useful and successful one. At all times keep in mind the purpose of the mentoring experience for students. The mentoring experience should be one that *provides the student with the necessary tools to make informed decisions about whether or not to pursue a particular profession.* Additionally, efforts to provide a safe and harmless encounter for the student must also be considered and in place.

## Mentor/Protégé Program Expectations

First, the assigned school personnel responsible for the mentor/protégé program needs to ensure that the mentor is willing to give his/her time to work with a protégé. Timelines for interactions with the student exist according to the schedule of the mentor. Considerations for the mentor's business hours of operation and times are set in place, so that he/she can conveniently provide the service without regrets. Second, the assigned school personnel should ensure that the *expectations* of the program are clear, concise, and understood by both parties. Third, the school personnel should meet individually with the mentor in the location in which the mentor's interactions with the protégé will occur. This provision provides an opportunity for mutual initial impressions between the school personnel and mentor to be established. Finally, school personnel remain present for approximately 15 minutes during the initial meeting between the mentor (professional) and the protégé (student). This provision for school personnel presence during the initial meeting may assist both the mentor and student to feel at ease during their first encounter. It also helps to start up conversations and "break the ice" when meeting someone new for the first time.

## Additional Duties of Assigned School Personnel

During visits of mentor/protégé interactions, the school personnel should be observing mentor/protégé interactions, taking notes about possible modifications for the program, and collecting data for a final report to educational stakeholders. This must occur in a manner that does not make the mentor feel that he/she is under a microscope. After all, the mentor is providing a service to the student and the public school system. If the mentor enjoys being a part of the program, he/she may be willing to provide the service again for another student. It is the responsibility of the school personnel to always keep the mentor informed about what to expect and what will take place during the program.

School personnel must explain to the mentor the purpose of conduct visits during mentor/protégé interactions. Again, the purpose of gathering data, information for surveys, and collecting suggestions by both the mentor/protégé for suggested program improvements. School personnel should explain that this information might be included in research presented to educational stakeholders to gain support for program continuation in the future. School personnel should offer to share the collected information and data with the mentor if he/she has an interest in the reported information. The offer to share findings or notes that the school personnel has been taking during visits is also an effective method to set the mentor's mind at ease or the removal of the perception by the mentor to mistrust the school personnel.

The final portion of the mentor/protégé program should provide an opportunity for the student to share a summarized version of his/her educational value, experiences, and current perception about the profession or field of study. The summary should also include mentor input and comments. This portion of the program gives mentor and protégé an opportunity to prepare for finalizing and sharing their experience with others. Suggested methods to share the experience with others are providing information about the program in a newspaper, special meeting luncheon with parents and invited guests, and all other participants in the mentor/protégé program. All participants have an opportunity to share their particular experiences and learn about the experiences of the other participants. If the program is successful in achieving its objectives for student learning and real world experiences, this will promote participants to talk about the experience throughout the community. What is the benefit of this accomplishment? This type of promotion serves as advertisement to get more business professionals to participate the next time. Below are three example forms for use in a mentor/protégé program. Once permissions on form one of four are completed, copy distributions of this form go to all of the following: school personnel, parents, mentor, and the participating student. In order to receive candid responses from both the mentor and protégé, the same information is present on form two of three in separate formats; one completed by the mentor and one completed by the protégé.

# Form 1 of 4 - Mentor Expectations /Protégé Responsibilities

<table>
<tr><td colspan="2" align="center">*School Name*</td></tr>
<tr><td colspan="2" align="center">*School Logo*</td></tr>
<tr>
<td>
Primary School Contact Personnel:<br>
Name and Title<br>
Address<br>
City, State, Zip Code<br>
Telephone Number with extension
</td>
<td>
Mentor Information:<br>
Business Name:<br>
Location:<br>
Address:<br>
City, State, Zip Code<br><br>
*Mailing address if different from above information.*
</td>
</tr>
<tr>
<td>
Alternate School Contact Personnel:<br>
Name and Title<br>
Telephone Number with extension
</td>
<td></td>
</tr>
<tr>
<td>
Protégé Information:<br>
Name:_____<br><br>
Area of Interest for post-secondary education:<br><br>
_____<br><br>
College/University of Interest:<br><br>
_____
</td>
<td>
Please check all that apply.<br>
Preferred Day    Preferred Time<br>
☐ Monday     8-11 a.m. ☐<br>
☐ Tuesday     1-3 p.m. ☐<br>
☐ Wednesday<br>
☐ Thursday    Other_____<br>
☐ Friday
</td>
</tr>
<tr>
<td colspan="2">
Note to Parent (s)/Guardian(s):<br><br>
The *High School Name* will be allowing students to explore various fields of future study through a Mentor/Protégé program. In order the your child to be granted the opportunity to participate, the *High School Name* will need to keep this letter of permission on file. By signing this form, you are agreeing that you are aware of your son/daughter's participation in the Mentor/Protégé program.<br><br>
Please check the appropriate boxes below, sign, and return to Primary School Contact Personnel listed above:
</td>
</tr>
<tr>
<td colspan="2">
☐ Parent(s)  ☐ Son          Date: _____<br>
☐ Guardian(s) ☐ Daughter<br>
Signature for Participation Consent: _____
</td>
</tr>
</table>

# Form 2 of 4 - Mentor Expectations /Protégé Responsibilities

| School Name | |
| --- | --- |
| School Logo | |
| Mentor Expectations:<br>1. Immediate notification if protégé fails to meet at the specified time.<br>2. Notification of School Personnel of any change in specified meeting dates and/or times.<br>3. Protégé's dress is appropriate | Protégé Responsibilities:<br>1. Dress according to the mentor's instructions.<br>2. Perform observation related duties as requested by the mentor.<br>3. Become as involved in learning opportunities and goal related experiences as legally allowed by the mentor.<br>4. Be on Time. |
| 4. Explain academic requirements for the profession to the protégé.<br>5. Suggest methods about how the protégé can begin preparation for his/her future goals while currently in high school | 5. Specific Goal Related Experiences Sought:<br><br>6. Previous growth opportunities in Field of Study: |
| 6. Provide school personnel feedback about the protégé's performance in the following areas of concern:<br>a. Attitude<br>b. Willingness to learn about the profession<br>c. Initiating questions of curiosity about the profession. | 7. Reason that you selected this particular Field of Study.<br><br>8. What would you do, if during the course of your participation in the Mentor/ Protégé Program, you find that you do not like the Field of Study? |
| 7. Be specific about what learning opportunities the protégé can expect by working with you.<br>8. Professional opinion about the student's realistic possibility of success in this profession. | 9. What learning objectives do you hope to gain through participating as a Protégé working under the tutelage of a professional in the selected Field of Study? |
| 9. Briefly, explain your ability to fulfill the objectives and goals as stated on the protégé's responsibility section of this form. | 10. Would you like to have the opportunity to have real world interactions or experiences with any of the following: Human Patients, Children, Others |
| 10. Would you be willing to allow photographs to be taken (under your specific guidelines and rules) for promotional purposes, advertisement, and about your participation in the Mentor/Protégé Program<br>☐YES ☐NO | 11. Would you suggest that other students participate in this program?<br>☐YES ☐NO<br>Please provide a short answer. |
| Comments/Suggestions | Comments/Suggestions |

# Form 3 of 4 - Mentor Expectations

| |
|---|
| ***School Name*** |
| ***School Logo*** |
| Mentor Name _____ (please print)   Date: _____ |
| Mentor Expectations:<br>a. Immediate notification if protégé fails to meet at the specified time.<br>b. Notification of School Personnel of any change in specified meeting dates and/or times.<br>c. Protégé's dress is appropriate |
| Academic Requirements:<br>Explain academic requirements for the profession to the protégé  and suggest methods about how the protégé can begin preparation for his/her future goals while currently in high school |
| Protégé Performance<br>Provide school personnel feedback about the protégé's performance in the following areas of concern:<br>   1  2  3  4  5<br>a. ☐☐☐☐☐ Attitude;<br>b. ☐☐☐☐☐ Willingness to learn about the profession; and<br>c. ☐☐☐☐☐ Initiating questions of curiosity about the profession.<br><br>I. Rank item a. using the following value system: 1=indifferent; 2=sarcastic; 3=blames others for shortcomings; 4=respectful to mentor and not others; 5=respectful to both mentor and others<br>II. Rank items b. and c. using the following value system: 1=shows no interest; 2= shows little interest; 3= somewhat interested; 4= interested but unrealistic perceptions; 5= interest level is high and has a realistic perception |
| Opportunities for Learning<br>Be specific, but brief about what learning opportunities the protégé can expect by working with you. |
| At or near the end of the mentor/protégé program, briefly state your professional opinion about the protégé's realistic possibility of success in this profession. |
| Would you be willing to allow photographs to be taken (under your specific guidelines and rules) for promotional purposes, advertisement, and about your participation in the Mentor/Protégé Program<br>☐ YES  ☐ NO (please check one) |
| Comments/Suggestions for Mentor/Protégé Program (improvement or deficiencies needing corrections) |

# Form 4 of 4 - Protégé Expectations

| |
|---|
| ***School Name*** |
| ***School Logo*** |
| Protégé Name _____ (please print) Date: _____ |
| 1. Specific Goal Related Experiences Sought: |
| 2. Previous Growth Opportunities in Field of Study: |
| 3. Reason that you selected this particular Field of Study. |
| 4. What would you do, if during the course of your participation in the Mentor/ Protégé Program, you realized that you do not like the Field of Study? |
| 5. What learning objectives do you hope to gain through participating as a Protégé working under the tutelage of a professional in the selected Field of Study? |
| 6. Would you like to have the opportunity to have real world interactions or experiences with any of the following: Human Patients, Children, Others |
| 7. Would You Suggest That Other Students Participate in This Program?<br>☐YES ☐NO<br>Please provide a short statement based on your answer. |
| Comments/Suggestions |

## Section 3 - Leadership & Education

# Chapter 8 – Action Research Study

## Leadership Role Assignment

E͡L͡.͡A The following action research study, Leadership Role Assignment and Student Motivation to Learn (Farlow, 2002) was conducted as my first attempt to discover if a student leadership development relates to academic achievement. The results of this action research study provided the initial information that later developed into the TMAE and FIP-2004. Using the FIP-2004 in conjunction with the components of the TMAE (later named Model of Excellence) not only provided sound evidence, but it also allowed refinements to take place through continued research. This action research study provided the initial tools needed to conduct scientifically based high school leadership development research in future studies.

The nation's leaders are constantly making choices about the need for international relations development, issues of keeping the interests of the United States safe, and various educational policies. These modifications are as a direct reaction to an ever-changing society (Karnes & Bean, 1995). Technological advancements are at the forefront of these changes. As technology continues to advance, the need for more competent leaders in society becomes even more apparent (Bennis & Goldsmith, 1997). When should character and leadership development for an individual begin? Early theorists suggested that individuals are born as leaders, but Hackman & Johnson (1995) stated, "Leaders are made, not born". Smith (1995) suggests that teaching students leadership skills and development occur in the public school system.

In order to develop as leaders, individuals need opportunities to lead (Gardner, 1990). Maxwell & Ziglar (1998) believe that everyone possesses the qualities of a leader. Conditioning for the desirable characteristics of leadership development begins in the home and can further develop within the school system (Covey, S. R., 1989). The individual undergoing leadership role transitions should not expect to find visual evidence of its existence (Smith, 1995). The real evidence of leadership becomes apparent based on the lifelong decisions that an individual chooses (Maxwell, 1999). Utilization of emotional resources equips an individual to make better life-sustaining choices (Payne, 1998).

The educational level achieved by an individual relates to choices made by the individual. Whether or not an individual is adequately prepared for a meaningful position in the future relies heavily on the goals set by the individual at an early age. Parents, public school educators, counselors, and administrators can be some of the first initiators of a student establishing goals for a successful future. If a student does not already possess a high level of self-esteem, self-discipline or the motivation to learn, the student will need assistance in the development of these characteristics (Lumsden, 1994). Payne (1998) states that the educator's role is not to save the individual, but to provide students with opportunities to learn. Gardner (1990) and Karnes & Bean (1995) attribute the role of responsible citizenship to youth leadership development. Once a student has acquired self-esteem, self-discipline and the motivation to learn, success is inevitable.

The purpose of this study was to determine if the assignment of a leadership role would contribute to a historically low-achieving student's motivation to learn. The overall goal of this study was to increase the level of self-efficacy, ability to self-regulate behavior, and motivation to learn for all of the students undergoing treatment. The participants in this study were 22 students enrolled in a regular chemistry class. The collected data for this study was the pre- and post-treatment quiz scores and survey results. The calculated F ratio value has a statistical significance of 10.51.

## Analysis of Variance for Leadership Introduction

| Variation Source | Sum of Squares | df | $MS_B$ | $MS_W$ | Mean Square | $\alpha$ | F value | F ratio |
|---|---|---|---|---|---|---|---|---|
| MS $_{Between}$ | 1613 | (K-1) = 2 | 806.5 | | 806.5 | .05 | 3.88 | 10.51 |
| MS $_{Within}$ | 920 | (N-K) =12 | | 76.7 | 76.7 | | | |
| SS $_{Total}$ | 2533 | (N-1)= 14 | | | | | | |

The resulting data validates the researcher's theory that as an individual's leadership skills develop, the ingredients of self-esteem, self-discipline, and the motivation to learn are all blended together promoting academic excellence for students. Sometimes an individual is willing to fail alone, but it is different story when that same individual becomes responsible for someone else. Students need to have an opportunity to become responsible for service to others. As a result, students will have learned one of the responsibilities of becoming a productive citizen. It is the belief of the researcher that the students' development as leaders will occur when they become more confident in their own abilities. The overall goal of the researcher conducting this study was to validate the concept that there is a real need for the implementation of rigorous leadership programs in the public school system.

The participants of the treatment group completed two leadership surveys: one before and one after treatment. These surveys measure the student's change in attitude. An additional pre-treatment includes the administering of a quiz completed by the participants. This quiz served as the baseline for post-treatment test and overall results of the study. Five students selected based on a science course failure in the past. Observed behavior, interaction with group members, and level of voluntary participation during classroom activities were areas of focus. The opportunity for these selected students to voluntarily participate, remain on task, or interact with other students during classroom activities were rare. The null hypothesis for this study was that there was no significant difference in a historically low-achieving student's motivation to learn once assigned a leadership role.

Terms and behaviors used in this study that may have a different meaning outside of the context of this study. These terms and behaviors are operationally defined as follows:

1. *Emotional resources-* being able to choose and control emotional responses, particularly to negative situations, without engaging in self-destructive behavior. This is an internal resource and shows itself through stamina, perseverance, and choices (Payne, 1998).

2. *Historically low-achieving-* students identified as a student at risk of dropping out of school, have failed two or more quizzes or exams during the class of this study

3. *Support System-* those individuals available and who will help. Support systems are not just about meeting financial or emotional needs; they are about knowledge bases as well (Payne, 1998).

4. *On task-* performing only those activities that have been prescribed by the researcher or group team leader.

5. *Off task-* performing any activity outside of those prescribed by the researcher or group team leader. Discussion of non-chemistry related topics within or outside of assigned groups or making comments for entertainment purposes.

6. *Voluntarily participate-* an individual raising his/her hand or speaking out to answer a question.

7. *Leader-* possessing an ability to influence others (Maxwell, 2001), taking responsibility for self and others, able to communicate ideas, self-confidence, integrity, and setting an example for others.

8. *Period-* a class period lasting for 55-minutes on a traditional school schedule.

9. *Combined minority population-* a total count of all percentages for the various ethnic groups within the school. The individual ethnic group percentages are as follows: 38.1% African American; 19.3% Hispanic; 6.4% Asian/Pacific Islander; and .7% Native American (TEA, 2001).

10. *IEP-* an individualized education plan is a document that states the modifications that a mainstreamed student with a documented disability must have in order to achieve success in the classroom.

# Method

## Participants

The participants in this study were students enrolled in a regular chemistry class. The participants in this study consisted of a combined 10th, 11th, and 12th-grade chemistry classroom consisting of 22 students. The basis for selecting this class is the students' similar academic abilities. The term student refers to the participants from this point forward. The group under study consisted of two students repeating the course, and 14 students who are students-at-risk. Also included in this group were: one student with an individualized education plan (IEP), one student identified as talented and gifted (TAG) in math, and four students who had no preparatory chemistry course. C. E. Ellison High School.

C. E. Ellison High School is located in Killeen, Texas a mid-sized city in central Texas (Greater Killeen Chamber of Commerce, 2003). C. E. Ellison High School is one of four high schools located within the Killeen Independent School District (KISD). KISD is centrally located between San Antonio and Dallas/Fort Worth, Texas. KISD is near the largest military installation (Fort Hood) in the free world. During the 2000-2001 school year, the enrolled student population at this school was 1,920. The student population is extremely diverse having a combined minority population of 64.5% (38.1% African American; 19.3% Hispanic; 6.4% Asian/Pacific Islander; and .7% Native American) and 29.9% categorized as economically disadvantaged (Texas Education Agency [TEA], 2001). The student mobility is approximately 27.9%. All stated results for this study are pre- and post-treatment.

## Procedure

A review of literature defining various characteristics of leadership, methods to help an individual develop the ability to make life-sustaining choices, advantages of allowing students to practice learned leadership skills, and leadership theories, an initial quiz was administered establishing a baseline. In addition to establishing a baseline, the scores for the students measure the effects of the introduction of the team leader role. All students completed an initial leadership quality survey. (Karnes & Bean, 1995; Bennis & Goldsmith, 1997; Smith, 1995; Burns, 1978; Maxwell & Ziglar, 1998; Covey, S. R., 1989; Maxwell, 1999; Gardner, 1990; Maxwell, 2001, Lumsden, 1994; and Payne, 1998)

# Leadership Quality Survey

For each of the following items, circle the choice that best describes you.

Gender:  Male        Female

Classification (grade):  10th      11th      12th

Read each statement and check the appropriate box that reflects your personal opinion.  A number of statements describing student attitudes and/or beliefs about leadership follow:

| | SA = strongly agree; A = agree; D = disagree; and SD = strongly disagree | SA A  D SD |
|---|---|---|
| 1. | I have opportunities to develop my leadership skills in the school environment. | ☐☐☐☐ |
| 2. | An individual or organization has helped me develop my leadership skills. | ☐☐☐☐ |
| 3. | Self-knowledge is directly related to my ability to lead others. | ☐☐☐☐ |
| 4. | A leader is someone who has the ability to tell others what to do. | ☐☐☐☐ |
| 5. | Leadership development at school can relate to global issues in the future. | ☐☐☐☐ |
| 6. | The following qualities are important for an effective leader: | |
| a. | Honesty | ☐☐☐☐ |
| b. | Competency | ☐☐☐☐ |
| c. | Admit their mistakes | ☐☐☐☐ |
| d. | Believes in the self-worth of others | ☐☐☐☐ |

The survey results establish a baseline measure of changes in attitude regarding leadership after the treatment.  After administering the initial survey, the students will receive short weekly quotes that defined the characteristics and qualities of a leader (Maxwell, 2001).  Near the end of the study, students will complete a second leadership quality survey.

# Leadership Quality Survey Results

| | |
|---|---|
| 1. | I have opportunities to develop my leadership skills in the school environment. |
| | Pre-treatment response        3-4= 31.8%; 1-2= 68.2% |
| | Post-treatment Response     3-4=95.5%; 1-2=4.5% |
| 2. | An individual or organization has helped me develop my leadership skills. |
| | Pre-treatment response        3-4= 50.0%; 1-2= 50.0% |
| | Post-treatment Response     3-4=95.5%; 1-2=4.5% |
| 3. | There is a directly relationship to my ability to lead others and self-knowledge. |
| | Pre-treatment response        3-4= 54.5%; 1-2= 45.5% |
| | Post-treatment Response     3-4=95.5%; 1-2=4.5% |
| 4. | A leader is someone who has the ability to tell others what to do. |
| | Pre-treatment response        3-4= 90.9%; 1-2= 9.1% |
| | Post-treatment Response     3-4=13.6%; 1-2=86.4% |
| 5. | Leadership development at school can relate to global issues in the future. |
| | Pre-treatment response        3-4= 50.0%; 1-2= 50.0% |
| | Post-treatment Response     3-4=100%; 1-2=0% |
| 6. | The following qualities are important for an effective leader: |
| a. | Honesty |
| | Pre-treatment response        3-4= 100%; 1-2= 0% |
| | Post-treatment Response     3-4=100%; 1-2=0% |
| b. | Competency |
| | Pre-treatment response        3-4= 90.9%; 1-2= 9.1% |
| | Post-treatment Response     3-4=100%; 1-2=0% |
| c. | Admit their mistakes |
| | Pre-treatment response        3-4= 90.9%; 1-2= 9.1% |
| | Post-treatment Response     3-4=100%; 1-2=0% |
| d. | Believes in the self-worth of others |
| | Pre-treatment response        3-4= 90.9%; 1-2= 9.1% |
| | Post-treatment Response     3-4=100%; 1-2=0% |

The duration of this study was approximately 22 days. The data collected for this study was the pre-treatment quiz scores, survey results, and a comparison of post-treatment quiz scores and survey results. Levels of significance were determined through analysis of results. Other forms of data such as observed behaviors, interaction with members of the assigned group and the level of voluntary participation are collected, but they were not the basis of this study. The followed pattern for this study was to teach a lesson, review the lesson, and give a written or verbal quiz the following day. Treatment of the group started on the third day.

During the first day of the study, the students used their periodic tables and received instructions on how to determine the electron configuration for specific atoms. Students had time for independent practice and a review of the lesson during the last 10 minutes of class. On the following day, the students stood around a representative periodic table drawn on the floor. Assignment of a timekeeper would announce when 15 minutes of class remained. Instructions to the students were as follow: Pay attention while each student demonstrator walked on the periodic table and called out information to his/her partner, try to find any errors that the partner wrote on the board, and to record the information in their notes. Observations were made of students asking each other questions about the demonstrations. Other student observations show students listening during answer explanation discussions.

According to the instructions given at the onset of this activity, students should remain actively engaged. Recording of student behaviors took place as students were demonstrating, observing, and interacting in activities. Demonstrator errors or misconceptions took place as needed. The researcher observed and recorded behaviors and activities of the off-task students. Some of the off-task students would glance up as they continued their various activities and conversations. Some of these students would laugh out- loud as they talked to friends. When the researcher suggested that students were not paying attention or were off-task, the identified students would point in the direction of the periodic table on the floor, pretending that they were watching the demonstrators.

Two female students pretended to be playing hopscotch by jumping to different tiles on the floor. Their game was the cause of many burst of laughter. One student watched activities on the soccer field from the window. The researcher heard students talking about upcoming football games and giving reasons why the winners would win. When the timekeeper called 15 minutes, all of the students returned to their seats. The researcher stated, "Clear off your desks of everything except the periodic table and something to write with." Some students commented that they were going to fail the quiz. One student commented that they had not reviewed for the quiz yet. The researcher explained that the entire class period was quiz review. This was the baseline quiz.

On the third day of the study, the treatment of the group began. The research listed explanations for possible reasons that students had failed the quiz. The researcher reminded them about how they failed to follow the instructions on the previous day. The students in this class received introductions to the activities and procedures needed to develop their leadership skills, and the researcher administered the initial survey. The students used a blank leadership quote form. Students received instructions on the method of recording the weekly quote. Each quote would fall into one of two categories: characteristic or leadership skill. The quotes were to be hand-written with the author's name. They would then place a check under the appropriate category. The weekly quotes continue on the same

70

form until all spaces are completed. The researcher told the students that some of the leadership quotes would appear as questions on future quizzes. Classroom instruction continued using the scheduled lesson plan.

Five students were selected, one from each group, to be the first individuals studied. The researcher observed student behavior, interaction with group members, and level of voluntary participation during classroom activities. The occasion for the selected students to voluntarily participate, remain on task, or interact with other students during classroom activities were rare, so team leader assignments went to these students. Once selected, the team leaders selected the other members of their group. The groups consisted of three groups of four and two groups of five.

The class and the selected team leaders received the instructions for the study. Team leaders were responsible for giving a daily grade based on the member's level of participation, contribution, and ability to stay on task. The team leaders received a grade based on their ability to perform these duties. This aspect of the study was included to validate the authority of the team leader to each member of the group. These daily grades were recorded in a separate grade book for research purposes only and do not effect a student's academic grade. The team leader nor the group members realized that the daily grades had no effect on the members' overall grade. Each team leader was also responsible for giving a daily report of their observations during the last ten minutes of class. The report was in reference to any concept that his/her group did not understand. The topics on the reports are the first items addressed the following day. A discussion and review session took place within the groups. Afterwards, a quiz is given. The researcher posted results of the surveys and quizzes so that students could compare performance and improvement.

During the study, the team leaders actively took notes, answered questions during discussions, reviewed and corrected their notes with their group members, and recorded weekly quotes. They also turned in reports of topics that their groups found difficult to understand, and turned in their recorded grades for group members. None of the reported team leader grades for group members fell below a 70.

## Results

The information obtained from these surveys assessed how each individual feels, believes and/or perceives the qualities of leadership. In addition to the before mentioned purpose, information from this survey was used to identify any changes in attitude based on the percentages of the pre-treatment survey and the post-treatment survey.

The initial survey took place on October 1, 2002, and all 22 students were present and participated in this survey. Administration of post-treatment survey occurred on October 30, 2002. Each participant responded to a series of statements by indicating whether he/she strongly agree (SA), agree (A), disagree (D), or strongly disagree (SD). An undecided/unsure choice does not appear as a choice so that each participant has to make a response that would fall in the valued or did not value scoring range. Each statement relates to a quality or characteristic of leadership. Each participant's score was determined by summing the point values of each statement. A score of 4 or 3 for a statement indicates that the students value the statement as a characteristic or quality of leadership. A score or 2 or 1 indicates that the students do not value the statement as a characteristic or quality of leadership. I have opportunities to develop my leadership skills in the school environment.

The percentages for the post-treatment survey results were significant and probably due to the weekly quotes and the discussions that followed. The students may not have made a connection with school activities and leadership characteristics or opportunities during the pre-treatment survey in statements 1-5. The percentages for the post-treatment survey for statement 6 were not as significant. This may have been due to the values that the students have about the qualities of an effective leader.

Use of a simple analysis of variance (ANOVA) procedure analyzed the pre- and post-treatment data. Comparisons between the pre-test scores before treatment and the post-test scores after the introduction of a team leader took place. Analysis of variance for each of the tests yielded the following results: The calculated F ratio value of 10.51 is greater than the F table, Table A.5 in Appendix A value of 3.88 (Airasian, P & Gay L. 2003). The calculated F ratio shows statistical significance therefore the researcher rejects the null hypothesis. A similar pattern resulted for the scores of the newly selected team leaders.

## Discussion

After two weeks, the original team leaders selected a new team leader within their established groups. The original team leaders then became a mentor to the new selected team leader. This process ensures that the new team leader follows proper procedures. Quiz and survey response data from October 1, 2002 until October 31, 2002 was gathered. This time span allowed inclusion of the second set of team leaders collected data. It was important to find out if this would give merit to the hypothesis. Does the assignment of a leadership role contribute to a historically low-achieving student's motivation to learn? The first selected team leaders were performing well, and it was difficult to switch them. They were having on-task discussions within their assigned groups, turning in reports of unclear topic content areas, and completing their assignments. It was also noticeable that these students were completing exam essay questions with more thorough explanations than they had in the past. There were higher expectations for the performance of these students, and they achieved higher scores as a result (Lumsden, 1997).

Burns (1978) names both self-esteem and social role-taking as two of the culprits that will either allow the development of young leaders to, or not to, occur. It was surprising to see the immediate transition in the attitudes and level of performance by the first group of team leaders. They took their responsibility and assignments as team leader serious. During the days of the study, students made on-task comments about the assignments. Group members encouraged the team leaders to ask questions when they could not answer questions after their collaborative efforts.

Some of the students in other periods began to inquire about the procedures implemented during the course of this study. Some of these students have been present in the library while the students under study were reviewing for an upcoming quiz. Some of the students stated, "These students seem real smart", and they joined in on the review session. There have also been two telephone calls from parents inquiring about how their child can become a chemistry team leader. The team leader assignment system is being used in all of the researchers other chemistry classes.

In order to confirm the effectiveness of the implementation of team leaders in the classroom, the researcher inquired with teachers about these students performance in other content areas. The results were consistent with those of the researcher. These students were striving to achieve higher levels of academic success. Mrs. Noteboom, a counselor at the high school stated, "When you assigned these students as team leaders, you gave them someone else to blame for their success. Sometimes the peer pressure is too great when students try to rise up to a teacher's high academic expectations."

## Future Implications

The public education system, currently undergoing an overhaul, is seeking methods to maximize student academic achievement level. Policy makers are taking a closer look at current educational guidelines and issues for schools, teacher quality, and student achievement. The term "accountability" occurs frequently in educational research and it seems to be one of the most reviewed terms in educational debates. The task of producing highly skilled and better educated students, future leaders of society, must be accomplished if American society intends to survive as a nation that other countries will want to emulate. Does this survival include the American society's ability to remain globally competitive?

Survival of this nature should not be a debatable one or dependent on the experiences, skills, and development of those currently in specific positions of authority.

Today's high school students have the ability to meet, perform, and excel at high standards and expectations when the provisions of proper training, guidance, experiences, and opportunities to grow as leaders are available for them. The results of this study have shown that a teacher having high expectations for students and an ability to convince students that they have the power and right to experience success will stimulate students to be self-confident in their own abilities. This is what it will take to assist students as they learn to recognize their internal power and become motivated to achieve successful results academically, socially, and emotionally. In the future, this research warrants further study in the area of team leader systems to validate its impact on student motivation to learn.

## Special Note:

While recently serving an administrator duty overseeing a volleyball game, a young man who had been a participant in this study was present. He was one of the original but somewhat reluctant team leaders. As we made eye contact, we were both surprised and delighted to see one another. This *"tough"* person hurried down the bleachers and gave me a big hug. What a wonderful young man he had turned out to be! Now a student at Central Texas College, he has his dream in clear view and is taking action to make his dreams become a reality. I found myself bubbling with joy as he told me what he had been doing since he had left C. E. Ellison High School before his senior year. Some lessons learned will stick with an individual for a lifetime and to provide some of these lessons is my intent. Later, as he sat up in the bleachers, I heard a noise coming from the bleacher area, he stated, "Get after them Mrs. Farlow, just as you use to get me", and we both just smiled.

# Chapter 9 – Motivating Students to Learn

## Energy Renewal

E<sub>L.</sub><sub>A</sub> Specialized science courses such as chemistry, biology, or physics classes did not exist in smaller school settings. Students learned a little about each subject under the title of science. It was fun taking periodic table quizzes on the symbols, names, and atomic numbers because great competitions against one another took place. The objective was to see who could turn the quiz in the quickest having the least number of errors on skeleton periodic table outlines provided by the teacher. Contests, competitions, and a worthwhile challenge stimulated student's ability to learn the material, and science was fun. However, memories of an actual course dedicated specifically to a college chemistry course were haunting. Memories of experiencing a panic attack and an elevated level of confusion when hearing the term *mole* as used by the chemistry professor were haunting also. Wondering if this was the correct science class, an image of a four legged, rat looking thing with dysfunctional eyesight, scampered around in my mind. I thought, "What in the world is this man talking about?" I realized that I had not learned one thing during the hour- long lecture because my mind was too full of questions and images of four legged creatures. As a veteran of the United States Army, a wife, and mother of two children, I could not dare ask my young 18 and 19 year-old classmates for assistance. After discovering how far off my thoughts became when I heard the word mole in my college chemistry class, I knew that I did not want anyone to have to that same experience.

As a secondary level classroom teacher, I frequently adjusted both my teaching and exploratory methods that promoted high expectations for academic excellence and successful educational experiences for *all* of my students. In 1998 during my first year of teaching, this system of belief became conditioned and became etched in my mind. Upon receipt of my first teaching assignment, I was excited about having the opportunity to share the secrets of chemistry that I had discovered while in college with my students. For me, these secrets unlocked the mystery of chemistry. I soon discovered that my level of excitement about teaching high school chemistry to my students did not necessarily equal their level of excitement about learning chemistry.

I used theatrics on a daily basis as I attempted to stimulate and get my students excited about learning. By days end, I would often be at the point of exhaustion. I began to believe that feeling exhausted at the end of the day was just a part of the teaching profession. One day, I watched my students as they quietly made eye contact with one another, as if to affirm something, and walked out of my classroom. I wondered what the glances meant. Continuing to watch them walk down the hallway, I noticed something. It was almost as if a bolt of energy suddenly shot through them. All of a sudden, they had a lot to say to one another as they energetically bounced out of view. Students talking did not amaze me, but the sensing their renewed energy levels as they left the class did.

I continued to stand in the doorway and observe as the students in my next class entered the room. They would say, "Good morning, Mrs. Farlow" as they entered the room. I returned the greeting still puzzled by what I had just observed. At the conclusion of the next class, I decided that I would observe these students as they left the room and walked down the hallway. As I observed the second class, I noticed a similar pattern; students seemed unmotivated about learning with a total loss of energy during class, but they came back to life in the halls. Later on during the day, I asked other teachers if they had noticed a similar pattern. Most teachers said no, while others implied that I should be happy that students are not as energetic in class as they became in the halls. I felt that some of the teachers missed the point of my question.

Later, I even noticed a similar pattern during labs. I thought, "What kind of students are not motivated about learning when they get to conduct labs?" Well, I discovered that several students lacked motivation about learning chemistry as well as their other content areas. I continued my investigation by looking in my grade book trying to establish a pattern, but I could not see a pattern. Some students achieved high grades, some barely the minimum, while other's performance remained unpredictable. I also discovered that when I asked questions that related to material that I had taught one or two weeks before, some of my students responded as if it was the first time that they had ever heard the material. I did not like what I saw, or the conclusion that I had drawn based on observations. I concluded that some of my students had little passion or motivation to learn chemistry. That was an unpleasant feeling, and I started to believe that I had just discovered my own motivation and passion for wanting to teach high school students. I decided that my mission as a teacher was to successfully provide motivational learning stimuli for all of my students.

A variety of initial attempts to provide students with motivational learning stimuli had proven unsuccessful ones. I soon discovered the correct mechanism that produced the potential to help me to achieve my goal. Within the new method, I began to uncover a secret about the motivation to learn factors of my students. I started to understand how students could achieve an educational ownership experience. I began to use special projects that offered students a choice about what they learned. I chose to use specific words as I explained the details and procedures that would allow my students to conduct a special project. I warned my students that the special projects would be very demanding and that they would have to show me that they were all capable of committing to the task. I discovered the importance of using words like special project, privilege, demanding, and commitment to stimulate the competitive nature in some students. Finally, I discovered that high school students were in search of learning opportunities that were unique, interesting, and allowed them to experience a sense of pride for what they learned. By the way, I started to see the same energy levels that seemed to only exist in the hallways before. Now high levels of energy were taking place in my classrooms as my students were actively engaged in learning with a purpose.

## C. E. Ellison High School Leadership Academy Founder

Mr. Rainwater established and founded the C. E. Ellison High School Leadership Academy idea to develop students as leaders. The original creation of the program was in response to negative involvement such as murder and other criminal activities by some of his high school students. During an interview that I conducted, he stated, "In order to reach students, the gap must be closed between high school and the real world. Academics in high school must have meaning for students." The legacy of establishing the C. E. Ellison High School Leadership Academy clearly belongs to Mr. Rainwater. As principal of C. E. Ellison High School, having the numerous responsibilities that go with that position, Mr. Rainwater was in need of someone who would help make his vision become reality. He appealed to the Killeen ISD Board of Trustees granted permission to fund the new coordinator position. During 2002-2003, two different coordinators held the new position. Neither of these two coordinators was able to establish the C. E. Ellison High School Leadership Academy as an effective organization. During the 2003-2004 school year, I became the coordinator. Would this year be any different? The answer was a definite yes.

I established goals and developed a plan to accomplish those goals. My goal was to establish C. E. Ellison High School Leadership Academy as an effective academic program that elevates the level of student success and academic achievement. My vision was one that would elevate Mr. Rainwater's original vision to a higher level and have the ability to effectively articulate and justify my actions through my student's accomplishments and continued research. It took a lot of dedication, persistence, and occasionally stubborn acts on my part to help develop the C. E. Ellison High School Leadership Academy into what it stands for today. The vision and mission statements of the C. E. Ellison High School Leadership Academy provided the organization with the focused purpose, goals, and objectives that it needed to become an effective program. I say, "Mission accomplished in 2003-2004."

# Membership

Membership in the C. E. Ellison High School Leadership Academy is available to students in grades nine through twelve. Member selection has four equally weighted criteria during the selection process. The criteria are as follows: Application process, teacher or self-recommendation, interview, and minimum grade point average of 2.75. In addition to the defined membership selection criteria, members are required to complete fifty community service hours, ten-hour minimum intern program, and mentor program that is often in conjunction with the member's original community service-based project. Members must also exhibit the eight values promoted by the C. E. Ellison High School Leadership Academy in daily living. The last four values were added during the 2003-2004 school year and are as follows: discipline, integrity, endurance, perseverance, compassion, empathy, humbleness, and a vision for future environments. I believe that the main objective for developing students as leaders is to provide them with unique experiences that inspire visions to become reality. At the same time, I believe that students need to have opportunities and detailed examples of how to success academically and in daily living.

## Missing Components

During the 2002-2003 school year, two different individuals had held the newly established coordinator position. Students were complaining about a lack of stability due to frequent changes in coordinators. Mr. Rainwater offered me the position of C. E. Ellison High School Leadership Academy Coordinator for the upcoming 2003-2004 school year. In January, at the time of the coordinator position offer, I had just started my Master of Education courses. I decided to take on a heavy course load so that I could complete the thirty-nine hour degree in twelve months. This was a personal goal. I was preparing for an assistant principal position within the Killeen Independent School District (KISD) after graduation. The Master of Education degree and a principal's certificate would allow me to hold an assistant principal position, allow me greater opportunities to have an active role in ensuring student academic achievement and success, and allow opportunities for me to become involved in the education decision-making processes.

During the next six-months, I continued to teach regular chemistry courses and the Advanced Placement chemistry course. I also completed graduate courses as a full-time student during the regular semesters and twelve hours during the summer months. I decided that I would take the coordinator position for one-year as I completed my graduate studies. As an elective course, I had selected the Organizational Management and Design course as my elective. While taking the course, I learned the importance of an effective organization to establish vision and mission statements. These two statements provide direction for the organization and a system to measure whether or not the organization accomplished its stated goals.

I spoke with two of my professors, Dr. Pamela Harrison (recently named as the Superintendent of Schools in the Temple Independent School District) and Dr. Peggy Malone (recently becoming the Academic Dean at Tarleton State University-Central Texas) about the C. E. Ellison High School Leadership Academy program and its potential to help students achieve academic excellence. I also spoke with them about its lack of organizational stability. These two professors were supportive in the efforts that assisted me as changes to the program took place, making it a more successful one. They were my mentors whether they knew it at the time or not, because I valued their experiences and expertise about leadership and how to motivate an individual to give his/her best. This is what they had motivated me to do. I later told them that I appreciated their genuine care, support, and ideas. These are two outstanding leaders who I will always remember in my "helped me develop" file.

In addition to the learning that I had experienced working with Dr. Harrison and Dr. Malone, I took an organizational design and management elective course that prepared me to successfully turn the fate of the C.E. Ellison High School Leadership Academy towards a positive end. The professor teaching the course allowed me to use the C.E. Ellison High School Leadership Academy as my organizational design and management assignment. While in this course, I learned to identify the components of an effective organization, and I focused my efforts on the components that were missing. During the remainder of the 2002-2003 school year and during the summer months, I worked to put the missing components in place so that my tenure as coordinator would be successful. As stated by Warren Bennis (2003), "The first basic ingredient of leadership is a guiding vision".

## Vision, Mission, and Culture Development

In the past, only selected members of an organization were aware of the organization's future goals and objectives. Those select individuals would protect the knowledge of that particular information from other members of the organization treating it as a big secret that only a few had the mental capacity to comprehend. The secret would be so big in their own minds that they failed to adequately explain the purpose of the journey. While this may be an exaggeration in most cases, the result was the same. Today, effective leaders recognize that in order to maximize organizational successes that everyone must know and "buy-in" to the goals and objectives of the organization; referred today as the organization's vision and mission statements. Why would anyone be willing to get on board and take a trip that has no purpose, direction, or promise of results?

I believe that it is important for a leader to adequately, and completely explain his/her vision to the individuals that have the ability to help him/her meet the objectives of the stated mission. When a leader truly has a "guiding vision", he/she will be able to explain the purpose of the journey to others. People are willing to give their assistance when they are aware of the purpose. If a leader fails to share this information, perhaps out of fear of sharing credit for the organization's success, the failure to properly inform may lead to the organization's detriment. Before I held the position of C. E. Ellison High School Leadership Academy Coordinator, I served as the selection and retention committee advisor for three years. I would ask specific questions about the program's intent or future goals and it seemed as if something more important would always come up. Finally, I interviewed Mr. Rainwater to get the information that I needed about his intent for the program. He stated the following:

The purpose of these activities is to develop leadership situations and hopefully the skills that will empower our students to be successful in high school. We do not ever take a kid and put him in a box. Instead we say hey, these are the needed leadership skills, develop these skills, it's going to get you where you're going. The mentorship portion of the program is critical to their success.

Now armed with new knowledge, and mission and vision statements in place, I set out to establish a standard set of goals, procedures, and guidelines for the C. E. Ellison High School Leadership Academy. I felt that important aspects of the program should focus on teaching students leadership theories, skills, and development; provide students with opportunities to practice what they had learned; provide students with unique experiences that aid in their development as life long learners; and solve real world problems through community service based projects. Using Mr. Rainwater's statement and my assignment both served to develop the mission statement for the C. E. Ellison High School Leadership Academy as follows:

C. E. Ellison High School Leadership Academy provides an academic program that empowers students by providing them with real world applications for a lifelong learning experience, develops student leadership skills and character, fosters high standards of academic achievement, and helps students to achieve future leadership success regardless of their area of interest.

Dr. Harrison assisted me in the development of a C.E. Ellison High School Leadership Academy vision statement. Using the eagle mascot as an acronym, the vision statement became: *Ellison Academy Growing Leaders of Excellence.*

What type of culture should exist in the C. E. Ellison High School Leadership Academy and one portrayed to others? Once everything was in place for the C. E. Ellison High School Leadership Academy (vision statement, mission statement, program goals and objectives), from my Organization and Design Management course, I realized that the culture of the program needed to be established. Lussier & Achua (2004) define culture as the aggregate total of beliefs, attitudes, values, assumptions, and ways of doing things shared by members of an organization and taught to new members. C. E. Ellison High School Leadership Academy members strive to maintain at a high level of performance, so the one selected according to Lussier and Achua (2004) were the characteristics of high-performance culture that follow:

- ❖ *Culture reinforcement tools* – ceremonies, symbols, stories, language, and policies.
- ❖ *Intensely people oriented* – members are allowed to excel and contribute, establish one on one relationships with members, exhibit dignity and respect to others, initiative and creativity in performing duties, reasonable and clear performance standards, mentor programs, celebrate achievements, rewards and punishment to enforce high-performance standards, increased responsibility for the best performing members, mutual respect and interdependency, responsible for the growth and development of assigned members, teamwork, higher morale, loyalty, and higher retention rates,
- ❖ *Results oriented* – limit membership to students who exhibit high motivation for success and achievement, ambition, and whose attitudes and work ethic mesh well with the C. E. Ellison High School Leadership Academy culture, time and resource investment in members who excel or achieve performance targets,
- ❖ *Emphasis on achievement and excellence* – policies and practices that inspire members to do their best and constructive coordinator and member pressure to be the best.

## 2003 –2004 Campus Improvement Plan Movement

I believe it is important to have a method to record the claims that you make about a program's accomplishments and successes. Without documented evidence to support your claims of success, individuals listening to you may think that you are grossly exaggerating or even lying. Documentation and measuring results of program intervention addition to my dreams soon followed because I did not want to fit into either of those categories. I found one major problem though, the C. E. Ellison High School Leadership Academy did not, and had not, used any real method as a means of maintaining data about the program. I decided that for the first time the C. E. Ellison High School Leadership Academy would have some established standards to measure its impact on the whole school.

At first, I just mentioned to Mr. Rainwater and the Susan Buckley, Curriculum Director, that I would like for the C. E. Ellison High School Leadership Academy to be included in the campus improvement plan (CIP). I offered to help develop some of the goals and objectives if needed. I thought that this would be enough since I had already explained to the importance of having documentation about a program's success or failure. Information of this type is vital in any organization, especially if the goal is success. Once problematic area identification has occurred, actions should take place to immediately rectify it and put the organization back on the right track.

As life would have it though, after a couple of weeks, I went back to check on the status of the inclusion of the C.E. Ellison High School Leadership Academy in the 2003-2004 CIP. Much to my surprise, consideration to include it did not even seem to exist. My blood pressure began to rise when I found out that the deadline to turn it in to the district was on this day. My blood started to boil when I found out that the Gifted and Talented program along with a new program both had goals and objectives already included in the CIP. Susan was trying to explain something to me, but I had already tuned her out. I started using my self-talk skills so that I would not say what was really on my mind, and I could see her lips still moving and motioning to something. All of a sudden, what I was *really* thinking, but I was still controlling and able to hold in a tiny spot in the middle of my throat, became stronger than I did. I blurted out, "No wonder no one takes the Leadership Academy seriously! No wonder people just see it as a bothersome club. The C. E. Ellison High School Leadership Academy is not a club it is an organization operating within the confines of the C. E. Ellison High School. No wonder no one outside of the school has even heard of the Leadership Academy. If I can't get support from the ones able to give it here inside of the school, my efforts to make positive changes any where else will all be in vain."

By the time that the words stopped coming out of my mouth, my tongue was dry and swollen, my entire head had became hot, and my nostrils became so flared that they blocked my view. I knew that I had to quickly leave her office because my voice began to tremble out of frustration and anger. I returned to my office and gave thanks that I would have time to get myself together because I didn't have any more classes for the day. While taking deep breaths to clear my head and relax, the telephone rang. I just listened to it as it rang. I had an idea about who might have been on the other end. I still could not talk to anyone at that moment.

After a little while, I checked my emails and there was a note there from Susan. She stated that she had been looking for me, so that we could work the situation out. When I went back to Susan's office, I had with me the current practice section that I had already written weeks before. Believe it, or not, I had originally written the current practices goals and objectives in case I was told that there wouldn't be time to include them. I gave Susan the tools that she needed to include them according to both district and campus goals and objectives for the school year (2003-2004). To make it even easier, I emailed a copy of all of the needed information to her, so that she could just cut and paste them in place. To say the least, the C.E. Ellison High School Leadership Academy and its members far exceeded all of the expectations (see notes section). As the C. E. Ellison High School Leadership Academy coordinator, I ensured the clear statement of program's goals to my students, their parents, and educational stakeholders both verbally and writing by including them in the CIP. This openly available inclusion for the program in turn, guaranteed the removal of confusion about the program and what the program did. My dreams for the C.E. Ellison High School Leadership Academy started becoming reality.

## Dreams Becoming Reality

Before serving as the C. E. Ellison High School Leadership Academy coordinator, I dreamed about an organization that had the potential to accomplish great things for its members. I dreamed of an organization that would allow students to develop the skills that would aid in elevating their self-efficacy, ability to self-regulate behavior, and become intrinsically motivated to learn resulting from their real-world experiences and opportunities. I dreamed that if these things would occur, students would be able to accomplish difficult tasks, act responsibly, and have a willingness to take risks by venturing into uncharted areas. I also dreamed about the development of a system that could record student accomplishments, growth, and development over time.

I have been referring to the C. E. Ellison High School Leadership Academy as an organization because it is a social entity, goal-directed, and has a structure that directly links it to internal and external environments (Daft, 2001). According to Gross (as cited Beach & Reinhartz, 2000) an organization can be regarded as a cooperative system giving it a reason to exist which in this case is educating and developing students as future leaders to ensure the stability of a democratic society. This organization's goal became one of developing responsible and accountable students with the reward of education ownership. Earlier I mentioned that the C. E. Ellison High School Leadership Academy has made a large number of changes resulting in students who have positively influenced the C. E. Ellison High School and surrounding community in the past year. I formulated three main reasons that the C. E. Ellison High School Leadership Academy had not fully developed into the organization that it had the potential to be. The reasons for the lack of development are as follows: *lack of commitment due to the absence of clearly defined goals; lack of both parental and community leader involvement; and individual's resistance to change.*

## Too Little Support

I realize that some of the accomplishments of my students seem hard to believe, especially for individuals who never had opportunities of these types while attending a public school. Not personally witnessing the accomplishments of the students of whom I am referring, stories about their abilities may sound far-fetched or even like a lie. It was for these and similar reasons that I was so insistent upon all of my students maintaining two versions of a portfolio. Authentication of the documents that each student maintained in his/her portfolio took place once Mr. Rainwater and I signed the documents. As an active advocate for student leadership development programs to be fully implemented into public school systems, I could not allow myself to fear hearing the word "no" as I continued to seek program support.

Through diligent efforts, I found the perfect recipe that developed correct skin thickness and consistency allowing negative comments about the likeliness of student development programs to exist in public schools to bounce off. I have also gained an understanding about the degree to which the development of this thicker skin protects against the rockets back blast because this research goes against the "grain" of societal expectations or the ideas widely excepted as the "norm" concerning public education. For example, I have contacted the websites of popular celebrity talk show hosts, someone from most major television stations, and a variety of news reporters seen daily on various shows about serving as an avenue for information dissemination about the benefits of student leadership development to the public, our society, and nation as a whole.

I believe that the accomplishments of my students can effectively serve as a method to stimulate a larger population of students to believe in and act on their dreams. These students have illustrated through their actions what possibilities exist when students are striving to do their best. Imagine a society of a majority of individuals view failing to accomplish a goal as a learning experience, opportunity for growth, or as a temporary obstacle. This is the manner that my students have developed about their ability to accomplish their goals. They also believe that are society's future leaders, and they are willing to prepare themselves to meet the challenges that lay ahead. My student's academic achievement, receipt of competitive scholarships, ability to effectively articulate their goals for the future, and student employment selection serve as evidence of what they have accomplished through effective student leadership development. Imagine the "jump start" that this would provide for all of today's youth as they continue to grow and develop into adulthood.

## What is the role of today's media?

I had always believed that the role of talk shows and the media was to provide the public with current information and serve as an avenue for legitimate information dissemination about real world issues. If the education that today's students are not a real world issue of concern, then perhaps someone should explain that to the individuals currently in public office and those who will be running for office in the future. Education seems to be a hot topic if one considers the multitude of times education flows out of individual's mouths during elections. Many individuals have stated, "A politician will say *anything* to get elected". That statement would seem to have great merit considering that public education, student achievement, and realistic measures that can resolve stated issues and problems have continued to be topics of discussion for years. The time is now for the public to take a stand and say, "enough talk already".

Individuals that hold key leadership positions in education need to receive a constant flow of heat beneath them to stimulate them to take legitimate actions toward resolving the issues of educating our youth. This heat must have a continued presence beyond the idea of providing students with educational goals that simply ensure a basic education. Is the standard of achievement to provide today's students attending public education facilities the widely and accepted "norm" by the majority of the American society? If this is the case, no one should act or be surprised to find that these basic goals have lead to individuals prepared for basic employment, basic preparation for post-secondary educational facilities, and a future society of individuals who dare not dream beyond the basics. Who holds the power to ensure that just providing a basic education for the majority of today's youth is not an acceptable standard? The answer for this question comes from the same individuals whose votes reflected the promises that they heard.

I realize that the individuals who work in the media are extremely busy and that receive many requests. Sometimes though, it almost seems like a large majority of news reporters and talk shows are guilty of waiting in the shadows for a sure thing to come into view. Once a network is daring enough to air something new, there is a pause, so that the other networks can wait and determine the public's response about the topic or a show that has just aired. If the new topic receives good ratings, then they all pounce on it and these acts make it the news. On the other hand, there are the shows with the focus about how Tom married Jane and cheats on Jane with her best friend.

People need to take time out, regroup, and refuse to have their intelligence pacified or insulted by this type of menial entertainment. American society already understands that the future direction of public education is everyone's business. However, many American have the belief that they do not possess the power that will promote change. This is not true. Think about the power in numbers. What we as a society watch, willing to accept as reality television programs, or refuse to watch is an effective method of getting the attention of those who can ensure that change does occur. Regardless of the resources that may exist for a select few individuals, we as a society must remember that a larger majority of individuals will attend public education facilities. The current public education system has shown an inability to support programs that provide a method to establish students as lifelong learners. Some programs have few methods that can provide evidence of how student learning today will carry over to activities outside of the public education setting.

What I do believe, however is that someone must be willing to fall into the "largely ignored" or stubborn category until they find a method to reach those individuals that are open to new directional goals for public education. Public education shortcomings are not the fault of teachers, standards of certification, administrators, or parents. The answer that has the ability to solve many of the shortcoming issues in public education is to effectively equip students who invite the opportunity to experience educational ownership. Public school's future must be considered interesting because it is everyone's business. At times, it seems that the only time you hear about public schools is when a teacher has had an affair with a student, or some other major tragedy occurs. This method of doing business must stop. Some of the political forums and the media can assist in getting the word out about public education programs or organizations developed to ensure that the Public School Provisions in State Constitutions are effectively accomplished. For instance, according to Alexander & Alexander (2001), the Constitution of the State of Texas 1876, under Article VII of Education Section 1 states,

A general diffusion of knowledge being essential to the preservation of the liberties and rights of the people, it shall be the duty of the Legislature of the State to establish and make suitable provision for the support and maintenance of an efficient system of public free schools.

The long-term benefits of many of today's public education reform efforts appear limited in scope. This limited scope often does not extend outside of the contexts of standardized testing providing a system of tracking state progress, reports, and assessments of the basic educational goals and objectives for student learning. I want the goal of public education to become the goal of motivating students to achieve their best, become leaders in action, become the owners of their educational goals, and become lifelong learners for my children, my students, and for society as a whole. After all, what do the words "basic skills" really imply? To me, basic implies that we as a society are willing to send our youth out into the real world unprepared. Accepting a basic skills standard is similar having a "sink or swim" mentality towards the education of our future society. This may seem okay right now, but who will be casting the majority of the votes for issues that affect us as individuals, or society as a whole. Individuals need to become serious about considerations for a revolutionary journey that provides a realistic promise for long-term results as a viable solution for student achievement and success. Public educational reforms must have the goal of implementing programs that provide education and service to students in a democratic society that extends beyond the doors of the public school building.

## Lack of Imagination

An individual's involvement in leadership training that is designed to groom post-secondary students or adults into effective leaders is not an automatic predictor for his/her ability to implement a successful student leadership development training in the public school system. One reason for this goes back to the two questions that I mentioned earlier and are still under debate by many: *What does leadership look like? What does a leader do that a non-leader can't do?* Now add the word student in these two questions. *What does student leadership look like? What does a student leader do that a non-student leader can't do?* For many individuals, regardless of their leadership backgrounds, answering these two questions in this context is difficult or even puzzling. I make this statement because as I was conducting my research, I contacted published leadership authors and universities designed to promote leadership development and they offered little, if any, information specific to student leadership development. I do not feel that the scarcity of information was due to indifference about the topic. I also felt that it was due to an individual's failure to ever consider the idea. Some of these same individuals did express their support and curiosity about student leadership development.

Few individuals can imagine their children or the children of others having the ability to visualize how they want their future environments to be and then possessing the will and skill to put it into action. This may be due to the fact that, some of today's adults lacked the necessary opportunities or stimulation that allowed them to dream the big dreams. Perhaps some of today's adults were capable of dreaming big dreams, but they had their dreams shattered by others who were not capable or imaginative enough to provide assistance and find the resources that would allow exploration of the possibilities. Do you still remember my definition of leadership? *Leadership is the process of developing the power to visualize future environments, a willingness to take part in planning, individual growth, and implementing necessary resources to make visions become reality.* It fits doesn't it?

# Chapter 10 – Lack of Organizational Growth

## Absence of Clearly Defined Goals

E.L.A. First, the lack of organizational growth was due to a loss of commitment since there was an absence of stated or clearly defined goals for the organization. I only learned of this need because of an organizational management and design graduate course. Establishing organizational goals through the development of a vision and mission statement served as the driving force for curriculum development, outcome measures of program intervention, and decisions guided by the value system of common goals to identify specific experiences or areas of responsibility for the members within the organization. Once in place, the organization has established its culture. Daft (2001) defines culture as the set of values; guiding beliefs, understandings, and ways of thinking that is shared by members of an organization and is then handed down to new members. The combination of the Theoretical Model of Academic Excellence and FIP-2004 can equip the public education system with a common set of tools to measure an effective leadership development organization, the organization's ability to measure levels of intervention, and the organizations ability to attain it's outcomes.

In a society that is constantly changing, students need to have unique opportunities and experiences that provide them with a competitive edge for college scholarships or employment opportunities regardless of their situational or environmental backgrounds. I want to have an active role in helping students believe that they can achieve their goals without trickery and deceit. This allows students to savor what they have accomplished without regrets. Our society needs to provide training, education, and experiences that will allow future leaders to avoid scandals and unethical decisions like ones made be some of the individuals or companies that we have all recently became so familiar with (Martha Stewart, Enron, mistreatment of Iraqi prisoners, Halliburton, and others).

Teachers and students must have opportunities to learn from the experience of setting realistic goals, understand what to do if they fall short of reaching their goals, and know how to measure the overall effects of goal attainment. They must also gain experience clearly articulating their goals, objectives, projected, and actual outcomes to others. How you may ask? Teachers should actively seek education, leadership, or business conferences and meetings that value the new information and knowledge. I remain committed to my dream that the public education system has the ability to develop students as leaders who believe that they have the power to positively influence their environments, one student at a time, the world will become a better place for all of us.

## Parental and Community Leader Involvement

Next, lack of organizational growth of the C. E. Ellison High School Leadership Academy was due to a lack of both parental and community leader involvement. The Killeen Independent School District, due to its location, is blessed. Fort Hood is bulging with talented people from a variety of experiences. The Killeen business community has shown their willingness to actively participate in the education and development of our students. With all of this available talent, all anyone has to do is ask for assistance. Most of the time, these individuals want to become actively involved and assist students as they develop, but they do not know what schools need or wants, unless someone is willing to tell them. Again, having and sharing the "guiding vision" will open doors for students that can lead them into a wealth of opportunities and experiences.

Warren Bennis (2003) refers to a leader needing to "understand stakeholder symmetry". I believe that stakeholder relationships need to be broader within the public education system as a whole. I have had the opportunity to express the need for our stakeholders to become actively involved in our organization through community presentations. I believe in the philosophy that "two heads are better than one" and the African proverb stated by Hillary Clinton, "It takes a village to raise a child". Stakeholder involvement allows students to work with a mentor in their area of interest and the internship portion of the program to thrive to new levels of knowledge and understanding the role of receiving a quality education. This gives students a powerful and lasting experience that will serve them well in their future endeavors.

All I had to do was ask for their assistance, expertise, or time. These individuals were more than willing to become involved in the education, opportunities, and experiences of these students. The result of educational stakeholder involvement provided members with numerous academic scholarships, opportunities to share their accomplishments in public forums, and recognition as effective leaders of the future that my students strongly deserved. Additionally, my students had opportunities to participate in local government activities, provide service and assistance to parents and children of soldiers who deployed to Iraq, and assist in making a difference for youth in Mexico (3 senior members) and Honduras (a freshman and a junior member). Instead of me actively seeking educational stakeholders to assist my students, the table was turned and they were seeking out my students due to their established reputations as reliable and effective leaders.

## Parents

I believe that parental support or a lack there of, can make the difference between a students ability to experience success as an individual, academically, and/or as a productive citizen.  I want the parents of my students to know and genuinely believe that I want them to be actively involved in the various activities of their child's public school education.  During my entire seven years of teaching, I have always been able to creatively promote an educational atmosphere where the parents of my students are involved in the education of our youth.  I do not believe that this atmosphere or the education contributions that parents are willing to make is realized by simply positioning them on the side lines or as spectators for various educational activities.  My doors remain open for the $C^3$ parent and community leaders (*curious, courageous, and confident*) whose experiences offer real world learning opportunities for my students.  I have always used parental involvement to assist student education regardless of the content areas that have I have taught (chemistry, integrated chemistry and physics, advanced placement chemistry, biology, or principles of leadership).  I believe that this is an effective way to establish ongoing and healthy relationships between parents, students, and teachers.  The experience of having this policy has proven beneficial for the parents, the students, and me.

Parents attended monthly meetings, parent-teacher conferences, all special events such as field trips, some served as members of the newly established Board of Directors, were actively involved as assistants for student projects, and they were patient and understanding as I fully implemented the entire program.  As a parent, I realize the strength that was required of these parents as they listened to their children complain at first about being placed outside of their comfort zones.  However, the parents saw differences in the children due to what they were learning and experiencing as members of the C. E. Ellison High School Leadership Academy, and they liked what they saw.  They also knew the long-term benefits for their children as they learned the skills that they needed and began to work through some of the less pleasurable experiences.

Parents of the students had first hand knowledge about my teaching methods and the reasoning behind the implementation of specific activities.  They felt welcomed and asked questions that helped them gain clarity about my research, goal and objectives for specific outcomes, and the expectations that I wanted my students to achieve.  Most of the parents that I had the opportunity to meet and establish relationships with acknowledge that I challenged my students to achieve his/her best performances. This actually caused conflicts within the family.  Some students, like other universal systems, wanted to exert as little energy as possible, but still wanted to obtain their desired results; success.

Stressful situations are a normal part of life and part of the key to success was for the students to develop an understanding of this fact.  Lifelong success occurs when students learn what actions to take to resolve or alleviate the problem that is causing them to experience the stress. I allowed my students to experience stress, but I was always there to help them as they discovered the methods to overcome the stress. I do not believe that my student's ability to strive for excellence and grow in their leadership abilities ever would have occurred if their parents or someone else had been willing to provide the answers for them. Parents also provided me with behavioral observations that they had made signally successful growth in either their children or other members of the C. E. Ellison High School Leadership Academy. A few parental comments follow:

## Mr. Richard MacNealy
Parent of Rachel MacNealy, junior member 2004-2005

I first heard about the Ellison High School Leadership Academy when my daughter applied to become a member at the end of her freshman year. As a former career military officer and now Vice-President of a $30 million corporation, I was excited that she had the opportunity to gain practical leadership experience while learning leadership theory under the tutelage of an educator who specialized in the field. After discussing the history, vision, and mission of the Academy with the school principal (Mr. Marvin Rainwater) and learning the specifics of the program from the instructor (Mrs. Angela Farlow), I recognized the tremendous potential the Academy held for our youth. As a result, I offered to assist, serve as a mentor, provide guidance, or participate in any manner appropriate to help students reach their goal. When Mrs. Farlow asked me to serve as a Board Member, I enthusiastically accepted.

During my first year on the Board, I had the privilege of working with students as they navigated the many challenges of leadership. Early in the year, their idealism and enthusiasm was palpable, but like all leaders, they encountered obstacles and suffered setbacks. Some became discouraged, which presented challenges to their peers; others learned that being a good leader also means knowing how to be a supportive follower. There were also those whose personal goals conflicted with the group's goals and others who had difficulty staying focused on their project goals. Each learned through their personal experiences and developed methods of coping with the challenges. Conversely, most students worked through the setbacks and achieved various levels of success. This rekindled their enthusiasm and provided positive reinforcement to their determination to persevere.

Mrs. Farlow interspersed leadership theory with the practical aspects of what the students were learning through their projects. She invited highly qualified guest speakers from the local community to make presentations covering topics as varied as the importance of personal financial responsibility to Maslow's Hierarchy of

Needs, Peer Pressure, Interpersonal Communication, Public Service, and many others. These sessions exposed the students to not only theory, but also to the speaker's practical experience in applying the theories in their careers, projects, and volunteer work of their daily lives. My experience with Ellison's Leadership Academy provided a glimpse into how our public schools, with the right vision and dedicated people, can provide positive, meaningful lessons our youth can use to make positive change in themselves and our society.

## Mrs. Kelly Barr

Parent of Lenna Black, senior member 2004-2005 and Jessica Black, sophomore member 2004-2005.

I never would have thought to ask for the summer research opportunity for Jessica with Dr. Embrey at Children's Rehabilitation Center if it hadn't been for my experience in the leadership academy. I wish I had this type of opportunity myself but I cannot afford the time off work for such because of finances. Jessica will have the opportunity during this summer to participate in a complete research project in her career interest, physical therapy, from conception to print, including the actual hands on research with a PhD PT who is well known and well published in the field of pediatrics. I asked him at a course he was teaching if she could visit for a week some summer before she enters PT school and he responded after lunch with the answer that he would prefer to have her for the summer and take her through a complete research project and offered he and his wife's home for living quarters. How generous and wonderful an opportunity but I never would have asked if the ideas of this type had not been a part of my experiences during Leadership academy. A PT school instructor said "what an opportunity. She will have all sorts of doors open for her when she applies to Pt school after that".

## Mrs. Alyson Hockenbrocht

Parent of Ryan Hockenbrocht a sophomore member 2004-2005

You know that I believe in the EHS Leadership Program! I believe that your expectations are very high, which makes students feel enough pressure, from you, to always be on their toes, and perform to the best of their abilities. Therefore, in my opinion, YOU are a big part of the reason that the Leadership Academy is so successful. I also believe that the students know that you truly take an interest in them as individuals, and that you are working to help them attain as many skills as possible to make them more successful, even "marketable" adults. You teach them how and why they should do many things that students, not in the Academy, have to learn for themselves, usually after they have graduated from high school.

What I am trying to say is that, take Ryan for example, he was very much of an introvert before he became a member of the Leadership Academy last year. He never initiated a conversation with anyone, and I know part of that is due to his hearing loss, but that was not the only reason. He had to gain self-confidence, which is exactly what he did while he was learning so many valuable life skills, in your program. As you offered him the opportunity to take on more responsibility, by becoming the 9th grade coordinator, he began to believe that if you felt he could handle a phone chain, and getting information to his peers, that he must have something to offer in the program. When he talked about his Leadership Academy meetings, he spoke with comfort, knowing that he was a part of the whole, part of a bigger entity, the Leadership Academy! Ryan is no longer rattled by an unexpected event/situation, he feels confident now that he can look at the situation and finds a logical and/or feasible solution.

The requirement of accumulating community service hours is such a plus! Now, to get into so many colleges, students need not only good grade point averages, but community service hours as well. Ryan has grown through completing his community service hours as well. He was worked at a health clinic, completing paperwork. At "Food For Families" Drive, worked for his church at a softball tournament serving at the concession stand and during Vacation Bible School. He has filed paperwork at the police department, helped at my school's carnival, as well as helping to plan and coordinate a summer book club at the Harker Heights Public Library. This has forced him to become a leader, even if he does not want to, as well as having to work directly with so many different types and ages of people.

In my opinion, the Leadership Academy is a "WIN - WIN" Program! Students, who have the drive to excel in the program, as well as their parents' support and encouragement, have no other choice but to come out ON TOP! When they go to college, they will be more prepared and mentally ready to handle whatever comes at them. After college, their vast experiences will help them to be the "Cream of the Crop" when applying for the professions of their choosing. That is what I think about your program! WAY TO GO! And THANKS so... MUCH!

Hugs,

Alyson

## Community Leaders

Full-scale changes occurred during the 2003-2004 school year for the C. E. Ellison High School Leadership Academy. These changes resulted in positive student experiences and outcomes for both C. E. Ellison High School and surrounding Killeen community. My ability to establish the C. E. Ellison High School Leadership Academy Board of Directors with the help and guidance of Mrs. Mary Kliewer over the summer months before the onset of the new school year was the beginning of these positive changes. The Board of Directors team consists of community leaders, business owners, a higher education leader, and a Judge. They have assisted in the effective coordination of this year's activities. According to Gross (as cited Beach & Reinhartz, 2000), an organization can be regarded as a cooperative system giving it a reason to exist, which in this case, is educating and developing students as future leaders stabilizing a democratic society.

As I learned new information, I implemented the learned information to its the fullest capacity. The courses that I had taken while in the M.Ed. Administration program, along with two female professors provided me with two outstanding mentors, and an opportunity to develop the necessary skills needed to effectively serve as the change agent for our organization. I worked with teams of individuals who had foresight for student outcomes from the lessons taught and personal experiences in the C. E. Ellison High School Leadership Academy. Together, we established of a dynamic culture and environment for student learning. I want the members of the team to feel that the "guiding vision" of the C. E. Ellison High School Leadership Academy is worth continuing after I have moved on.

The 2004 activities, accomplishments, and established support systems have established the precedent for the C. E. Ellison High School Leadership Academy. Diligent service to the vision, mission, and purpose of the C. E. Ellison High School Leadership Academy have shown students how to make their dreams become realities. This only occurred through the concerted and active efforts of all of Killeen's educational stakeholders. Business owners, community leaders, and parents in the city of Killeen are active participants in providing learning opportunities, serving as mentors, and in the education of students. For example, Mrs. Mary Kliewer, parent of an original member of the program six years ago and a current member, is a successful businessperson and the co-owner of Patriot Cars, one of the largest car dealerships, in Killeen, Texas. Mrs. Kliewer serves on a variety of education and community boards. The summer before the 2003-2004 school year, she worked with me and guided me to individuals that would be willing to assist me in accomplishing our newly established goals for the C. E. Ellison High School Leadership Academy. Mrs. Kliewer's guidance and mentorship was instrumental in the C. E. Ellison High School Leadership Academy Board of Directors establishment. The newly formed Board of Directors consisted of community leaders, business owners, and a Judge. Additional examples of community leader involvement follow:

Mrs. Kelly Barr, parent of members Lenna and Jessica Black, business owner of Kidz Therapeze. She is also an active member of the Killeen Rotary Evening Club. She was instrumental in promoting academic scholarships and leadership opportunities for C. E. Ellison High School Leadership Academy members. Mrs.

Barr also provided constructive criticism to improve the program even more for the upcoming 2004-2005 school year.

Mrs. Brenda Coley, Secretary, Killeen ISD Board of Trustees, CEO of Human Resource Development at Metroplex Hospital in Killeen, Texas. Mrs. Coley has provided program input, feedback, and support as a member of the C. E. Ellison High School Leadership Academy Board of Director and on a community leader level. For example, a member of the program in 2002 returned to the C. E. Ellison High School Leadership Academy to get copies that she needed from her TAG Executive notebook. While she was there, she looked around and talked about all of the changes that had occurred. Proudly, I showed her the logo that included the vision statement that students had painted on a wall during the spring break. This former member was amazed.

We continued to talk and I asked her what she was currently doing. She stated that she was searching for a job as a radiology technician. She had received training for this job as a recent graduate in the Army Reserves. I told this student about the one of the C. E. Ellison High School Leadership Academy Board of Directors who was also the CEO of Human Resource Development at the Metroplex Hospital. I asked this returning student if she would like me to try to assist her in her job search. Quickly, I heard a somewhat surprised, but excited, yes reply. I called Mrs. Brenda Coley and explained the student's situation. We set up an interview time for the returning graduate. Not really knowing this student on a personal level, I felt that I had a good understanding of her through our conversations. I asked the student if she would like me to go to the interview with her and introduce her to Mrs. Coley. Again, her reply was yes! Mrs. Coley gave the student feedback about her resume, and set up a job interview for the student with the director of radiology. Guess what? The student got the job.

**Note:**

Mrs. Coley is currently the President, Killeen ISD Board of Trustees for the 2004-2005 school year, and she will resign as a C. E. Ellison High School Leadership Academy Board of Director member due to the additional duties and responsibilities of this new position. She is a major asset to the Killeen Independent School District and Killeen, Texas community as a whole.

Mr. Richard MacNealy, parent of member Rachel MacNealy, a retired Lieutenant Colonel in the U.S. Army who is now a contractor for S[3] Inc. for the U.S. Army at Fort Hood, Texas. Mr. MacNealy provided input for the program, provided interpersonal skill development presentations for members, staff, and advisors.

These C. E. Ellison High School Leadership Academy Board of Directors provided active involvement, service, and were instrumental in the effective coordination of the 2003-2004 school year's activities and successes. Through determined and combined efforts of all of these individuals, the C. E. Ellison High School Leadership Academy's focus and goals became clear and understood by all of the stakeholders (KISD, students, parents, community members, teachers, staff, and partners). Together the Killeen educational stakeholders and C. E. Ellison High School Leadership Academy accomplished unmatched greatness and opportunities for student leadership development and growth during the 2003-2004 school year. The students who participated in these experiences will have something positive to look back for a lifetime.

## Resistance to Change

The final reason that there had been a lack of organizational growth in the C. E. Ellison High School Leadership Academy was due to individual's resistance to change. While serving the organization as the selection and retention committee advisor in 2000-2003, I developed ideas of change that I believed would help the C. E. Ellison High School Leadership Academy become a fully functioning organization within C. E. Ellison High School. Although my ideas largely ignored and viewed as too idealistic, I never allowed my dream to become shattered. Instead, I began to conduct action research within my chemistry classes. I wanted to determine if my theory was correct about giving students opportunities to serve as leaders would motivate them to become students who were responsible, accountable, and strive to achieve their academic best. I later developed the *Theoretical Model of Academic Excellence* now redesigned as the Model of Excellence (ME). When the prospect of change becomes real, some individuals openly make statements similar to these, "We've never done it that way before." or "What if it doesn't work?"

Often times, delays in finding effective solutions result from fear of failure. I believe that this type of mindset places limits on an individual's ability to fully recognize or accomplish his/her dreams, ambitions, and goals. I refuse to live my life attempting only the sure things or those that I already know how the situation will play out. Matter of fact, I believe that very few situations give rise to sure things. Curiosity and the desire to find a new solution for an age-old problem are both precursors to new discoveries. I enjoy exploring the unknown and I gain fulfillment-accomplishing things others say are impossible. That is how my passionate belief about student academic achievement and success developed. I believe that is has more to do with the student's ability to believe in self than it does with anything else. It is not enough to state, "I believe in you, or I believe that you can do it." A student's personal experiences and that promote growth and success will affirm the student's belief system in his/her true abilities. Without real world experiences and exploration opportunities, students have no real way to measure or test their true ability to accomplish a task.

In order for this to occur at its fullest extent, educational leaders and policy makers need to keep open minds and brace themselves for the powerful effects of its outcome. Students believing and taking action to influence their environments holds great benefits for adults who interact with students like these. If educational leaders and policy makers are able to have the experience of witnesses first hand the true power that comes from within student who have undergone real and intense leadership development training, they cannot help but view it as a possibility for a revolution in the public education system. This new discovery of using student leadership development as a means of student achievement provides a mechanism for students to dig deep into the confines of self and pull out the formula for their own successes now and later in the future.

When I have committed to a task, I see it through to the end. I believe that individuals on a mission must exhibit unwavering dedication and perseverance in order to accomplish a difficult task. This is often difficult, especially if the proper level of support by those in charge of finalizing decisions is absent or subject to change as if moving in harmony with the tide. Some members of C. E. Ellison High School faculty, not serving as advisors, viewed the C. E. Ellison High School Leadership Academy program as a method of developing students within an elitist culture, environment, and/or attitude. This often times a freely vocalized opinion expressed by certain types of individuals when the topic of discussion is leadership, or student leadership. These individuals make an association of leadership with the markings of the elite. They also fail to realize that the absence of an effective leader who is dedicated to the leadership development of others leaves an avenue for chaos erupt regardless of the particular environment (educational or non-educational).

However, when an effective leader's goals are to assist in the leadership development of others, and he/she is capable of clearly articulating these intentions, stating the established goals, others members of the team will "buy in" to the concept. In addition to others buying in to the concept, an effective leader also knows the importance of his/her team establishing a common set of values, ethics, belief systems, and standards that the team members believe are important; this may also be referred to as the rules and guidelines of the team/organization. The effective leader then ensures equity in the ability for all members of the team to adhere to these established rules and guidelines. Once established, the team moves forward accomplishing their goals as stated and positively influence their environment. Are these same individuals as vocal about acts of this type? Probably not. The actions of an effective leader do not fit into a predefined leadership schema.

# Support Gains

After endless attempts to gain the support of other teachers within C. E. Ellison High School, I concluded that individuals outside of C. E. Ellison High School tended to be much more receptive and supportive to the C. E. Ellison High School Leadership Academy member's needs. Some of the teachers had been teaching at C. E. Ellison High School for a number of years. These type teachers tended to forget that the members C. E. Ellison High School Leadership Academy were still students under construction and development, so to speak. It almost seemed as if they thought that student membership in the program equated to perfection. Some of them behaved as if they thought that these students should be incapable of making an occasional poor choice or decision. If a student made a poor choice about turning in an assignment or was just being a normal teenager, these teachers were willing to publicly denounce the organization as a whole.

When negative teacher comments or opinions spilled over into action against my students on a personal level due to a poor choice or the act itself, I would quickly address the situation with the teacher and remind them that we all make mistakes. I hold firm to the belief system that individuals must be accountable for their actions. Corrective actions for poor choices must address correcting the underlying or obvious factors of the poor choice or act without dehumanizing the student. I try to put myself in the shoes of the student in order to gain an understanding from his/her perspective. Some adults either do not know how to do this, or choose not to do it based on a lack of care. I had to equip my students with the knowledge that their constitutional rights were not lost when they entered into the public school building. My actions and ability to invoke the thought processes for some of these teachers were not always popular ones, but many of them soon realized that the mission that I was on was not one desiring to win a popularity contest. Without my intervention at times, the negativity would have spread throughout the entire school system like an untreated viral infection.

At first, I ignored that type of teacher realizing that I did not have the power to change them. I soon realized that my original thoughts were in error. I was not trying to change the individual; I only wanted to change his/her perception about the members, goals, and objectives of the C. E. Ellison High School Leadership Academy. With this new thought firmly in place, I began to do this by developing ways for the C. E. Ellison High School Leadership Academy to affect a greater population of non-member students and teachers within C. E. Ellison High School. As I began to focus on changing the perception of some of the teachers, I realized that I had a variety of teachers and staff that formulated their perceptions about the organization due to a lack of properly articulated goals and objectives. When something seems to be a well-kept secret, individuals will often speculate about what the secret is about or what it does.

Sharing information with the teachers and staff about the C. E. Ellison High School Leadership Academy's goals and objectives had been impossible before the 2003-2004 school year because they were non-existent up to that point. No wonder the individuals involved in the program in the past had seemed reluctant to share information. They did not know it to share it, so a new mission arose. It became one to change the lack of an ability to share information about the C. E. Ellison High School Leadership Academy. These goals for change resulted in C. E. Ellison High School faculty and staff support and program perceptions also changed. Supportive comments follow:

## Mrs. Tami Kraft

Teacher: Humanities
Program Advisor: 2002-2003 and 2003-2004

According to Barbara Clark in her book *Growing Up Gifted*, gifted and talented students have an "advanced cognitive and affective capacity for conceptualizing and solving societal problems." When a student sees a problem that could improve their school, their community or even their world, they must be encouraged to act. Without action, these students will become frustrated and may give up on their ability to make a difference in the world. "Lack of opportunity to use this ability (leadership ability) constructively may result in its disappearance from the child's repertoire or its being turned into a negative characteristic."

The C.E. Ellison Leadership Academy empowers students to accomplish a goal that is impossible for an individual to complete alone. Community groups, faculty advisors, and other students ensure that any student can achieve their goal while following accepted protocol. Students learn how to make change within the guidelines of a bureaucracy. One of the greatest lessons is that corporations and community organizations must work within their own guidelines and cannot give immediate answers most of the time.

In the school setting, students often procrastinate and turn in a project at the last minute. When change in a community is involved, even something a simple as putting up an electronic message board, time must be managed well. Nothing can be accomplished at the last minute. The Leadership Academy allows students to fail. No one forces students to follow the timeline they set for themselves. No one will make the phone calls, write the letters, or communicate in a timely manner for the student. The Academy teaches students about true teamwork, when to ask for help, and the need for others to make a change in the world.

The Leadership Academy provides opportunity for the student to work on solving a problem they see in the world. Even without success, the students see how they have made a difference, what they can do better next time they try to make a change, and have honed some valuable leadership skills. For many students, the projects they attempt for the Leadership Academy demonstrates to them the difference between destructive and constructive criticism. Encouragement with criticism primes the student to take on another challenge or to make a fresh start at completing their original goal. Destructive criticism makes a student want to quit.

## Mrs. Phyllis Ferguson

Secretary: Finance

Note sent to Mrs. Farlow:

I just wanted to let you know what a pleasure it has been to work with your Leadership Academy students this past year. I know they were potential leaders prior to participating in the program at Ellison High School, but the material they learned and the student projects they tackled helped them polish and perfect their skills. The students I met were always courteous, and appreciative of the smallest gestures of assistance. I especially enjoyed receiving a postcard from one student attending a student leadership conference this summer. These students are caring, involved and intelligent. It has been a joy to help them this year, and I would love to be available to them, and continue our friendship as they leave Ellison. Truly, Phyllis Ferguson

## Section 4 - Dreams for The Future

# Chapter 11 – Educational Insight

**The Future Dreamers**

E<sup>L</sup><sub>A</sub>ducational programs holding promise for ensuring the academic success and achievement for all students through leadership development remain in small "pockets" of society. They almost seem a sort of anomaly that only occurs within specific communities. An example of this is the Leadership Training Institute (LTI) at John F. Kennedy High School located in Silver Spring, Maryland. In a telephone conversation with the Director of the LTI program, Greg Bowman stated, "It is very difficult to get the word out about the need for student leadership development research" (G. Bowman, personal communication, February 27, 2004). C. E. Ellison High School Leadership Academy modeled its original curriculum using the LTI program because so few student leadership programs exist.

Educational programs holding the promise of raising expectations for academic achievement must provide students with opportunities, and experiences that will allow students to recognize their ability to transfer of what is learned into other settings. *A student's combined development of leadership skills, self-efficacy, self-regulation, and intrinsic motivation resulting from the community service-based project will lead to students who are self-directed life long learners.* It is likely that these students will set the bar for expectations at the mastery level for all other encounters. Senge (1990) described personal mastery as the cornerstone of success. By definition, mastery is having an ability to possess or a display of great skill or knowledge (Merriam-Webster's Collegiate Dictionary, 1998).

Hilda Taba quotes a statement made by John Dewey in 1897 (as cited in Schultz, 2001): "An endeavor to shape the experience of the young so that instead of reproducing current habits, better habits shall be formed, and thus the future adult society be an improvement on their own…We are doubtless far from realizing the potential efficacy of education as a constructive agency of improving society, from realizing that it represents not only a development of children and youth but also of the future society of which they will be the constituents." The statements made by Dewey in 1897 are still prevalent issues in the education of students today. Beginning student leadership training at the secondary level within public schools provides a multitude of advantages for the students undergoing the training. This is true; as long as those implementing the student leadership development have, themselves received effective leadership training.

## A New Discovery

In addition to the development of the TMAE and FIP-2004, I began to realize that the actions and results that I was getting out of my students did not fall into the "norm" for high school student performance. Through reflections, discussions, and observations of my students by their parents, teachers, staff, and adults that interacted with these students, I realized that I might have discovered something else. Something that was unintended. What was it that made some of my students so different from other students? Why did my students seem to stand out in a crowd because of their accomplishments and their visions for the future? I experienced an "ah ha" moment. Could it be that most of these students do not fall into a normal category, because a category describing the ability of students capable of performing at this level is unique? Could these students fit into that category that is the most widely underserved at both state and national levels? Could the students be gifted and talented in leadership? I then turned my focus to the attention of research that related to students identified as gifted and talented in leadership. Can you guess what I discovered? Right, not much. I did find articles by well-respected researchers in the gifted and talented field, but even these researchers failed to give a definition of leadership or a description of what students are capable of doing when placed in the category of students gifted and talented in leadership.

Leadership has been included in the federal definition of gifted and talented since 1972 (Karnes & Bean, 1990). In 1995, the 74th Legislature of the State of Texas passed the Texas Education Code, Title 19, Part II for *Educational Programs for Gifted and Talented Students* and the subchapter § 29. 121, provide the definition of the "gifted and talented student" (Texas Education Agency [TEA], 1995). Since this is the case, why is it that no state or federal guidelines or measurements exist specifically for student identification in the leadership gifted and talented category? According to the definition of the Texas Education Agency (1995), a gifted and talented student means a child or youth who performs at or shows the potential for performing at a remarkably high level of accomplishment when compared to others of the same age, experience, or environment and who: exhibits high performance capability in an intellectual, creative, or artistic area; possesses an unusual capacity for leadership; or excels in a specific academic field.

Renzulli (1998) defines gifted behavior displayed by creative and productive persons as being the result of interaction among three clusters of traits: being above average but not necessarily superior ability, task commitment, and creativity. Gardner (2003) defines intelligence as the way in which one carries out a task in virtue of one's goals. Paul Torrance, creativity pioneer, founded the Future Problem Solving Program (FPSP) a program that stimulates critical and creative thinking skills and encourages students to create a vision for the future (Future Problem Solving Program, n.d.; Hébert, Cramond, Millar, & Silvian, (2002).

A closer look into the visions that some of these students have brought into the real world not only defines gifted and talented leadership, but it also provides insight about what these students are capable of accomplishing with the proper guidance and empowerment. Reflection on their experiences will allow students to modify their behavior and embrace their desired goals. Having opportunities to practice and refine the skills of self-regulation will lead an individual to experience an elevation of self-efficacy. As I stated earlier, an individual is now equipped with the tools to become intrinsically motivated to accomplish specific goals or to become risk takers in novice situations which will provide greater success ratios in their future endeavors. My definition of leadership paints a visual image and provides a sense of accomplishment by students who are gifted and talented leadership. The common set of twelve attributes that I have identified as unique for students gifted and talented in leadership based on observations, FIP-2004 results, community service based project completion, and senior member project scores. The attributes of students gifted and talented in leadership are: vision, passion, mission, compassion, reflection, perseverance, empathy, new creations, intrinsic motivation, success, responsibility, and accountability.

## Identification of Students Gifted and Talented in Leadership Scale (ISGTL-Scale)

The attributes of students gifted and talented in leadership and student leaders are: Vision, Passion, Mission, Compassion, Reflection, Perseverance, Empathy, New Creations, Futuristic Perspective, Success, Intrinsic Motivation, and Accountability. The common set of twelve attributes that I have identified as unique for students gifted and talented in leadership and student leaders based on all of the following:

- ❖ Student observations;
- ❖ Model of Excellence variables;
- ❖ FIP-2004 results;
- ❖ Community service based project completion
- ❖ Student's ability to complete all of the project guidelines as outlined in the Community Service-Based Project Criteria; and
- ❖ Completion of the Project Guidance Worksheet.

| Stages I-IV: 12 Attributes of Students Gifted and Talented in Leadership | | |
|---|---|---|
| Stages | Timeline | Attribute Measurement |
| I | October | Vision, Passion, and Mission |
| II | December | Compassion, Reflection, and Perseverance |
| III | March | Empathy, New Creations, and Futuristic Perspective |
| IV | May | Success, Intrinsic Motivation, and Accountability |

Operating under the premise that a student's *basic skills* development has occurred before they entered into a high school setting. An initial evaluation of the student's basic skill assessment takes place. The initial basic skill assessment occurs during oral and written assignments, individual and group presentations, and hands-on activities. Once evaluated, student needs for further basic skill development tailoring occurs throughout ongoing training opportunities. Basic skill development for students is not a focus of the ISGTL-Scale. However, students will have the opportunity to further develop their basic skills in areas needing improvement throughout implementation of the Eight Phases of the Model of Excellence. Leadership reception of information assessment and evaluations take place as students learn the various leadership theories, principles, and applications. The basic skills follow:

| Basic Skills Not Included in the ISGTL-Scale | |
|---|---|
| Communication skills | Problem solving skills |
| Critical thinking skills | Commitment |
| Decision-making skills | Follow-through skills |
| Teamwork | Understanding of Empowerment |
| Setting the Example | Time management |
| "Outside the Box" thinking skills | |

## Farlow Instrument Package –2004 (FIP-2004)

I. Contents Include

Introductory Information

Program Coordinator Items

Student Items

References

II. Program Coordinator Items

This section includes the following:

Sample Forms 1 and 2 that used according to student or program coordinator preference.

Scoring Explanations with Examples

Note to the Program Coordinator

Instructions Section

Identification Of Students Gifted And Talented In Leadership Scale (ISGTL-Scale)
Stages I-IV of the ISGTL-Scale Timeline
ISGTL-Scale Stages I-IV
Community Service-Based Project Criteria
Project Guidance Worksheet
Mentor/Protégé Information, Criteria,
Project Symposium Participant Survey
Leadership in Action Questionnaire
Model of Excellence
Project Success Analysis
Stakeholder Survey
III. Student Items (Each stage of assessment will include student self-analysis, peer observation analysis, and teacher analysis with comparisons between the three forms of analysis are noted).
1.   Identification Of Students Gifted And Talented In Leadership Scale (ISGTL-Scale)
Form 1:  ISGTL-Scale: Stage I
Form 2: ISGTL-Scale Stage I
Form 1: ISGTL-Scale Stage II
Form 2: ISGTL-Scale Stage II
Form 1: ISGTL-Scale: Stage III
Form 2: ISGTL-Scale Stage III
Form 1: ISGTL-Scale Stage IV
Form 2: ISGTL-Scale Stage IV
2.   Community Service-Based Project Criteria Checklist
3.   Project Guidance Worksheet
4.   Leadership in Action Questionnaire
5.   Project Success Analysis
6.   Stakeholder Survey

# FIP-2004 Sample Item #1

School Letter Head                                                    Logo

Community Service-Based Project Criteria Checklist

Status of Project's Progress  [Completed =X;  Incomplete = /]

1. Project vision and mission statement development
☐

2. Posters and brochures produced for project advertisement
☐

3. Invitations sent in a timely manner to all stakeholders
☐

4. Project procedure notebook developed,  maintained and updated
☐

5. Project data and presentation maintained in electronic portfolio
☐

6. Reflective learning experience documented
☐

All Required Forms Completed

a. ☐Project Worksheet                    f. ☐Leadership In Action Survey

b. ☐(2)Electronic  Portfolio            g. ☐Project Analysis

c. ☐Self-Directed  Learning Inventory   h. ☐Project Data Analysis

d. ☐Project Guidance Worksheet          i. ☐Data Visual Graphics

e. ☐PowerPoint ®Presentation            j. ☐Positive/Negative Experience

                                        Date:_____
Project Title:_____
Board of Director Proposal Date:_____

Name:_____

# FIP-2004 Sample Item #2

School Letter Head                                            Logo
Project Guidance Worksheet

Project Title_____

Name(s) of Primary Project Coordinator_____

Name of Secondary Coordinator_____

Community Leader involvement ☐Yes or ☐No
1. Environment Impacted by the Project (check appropriate box):
☐Internal (within School)
☐External (surrounding community or city)

2. Project:
a. Purpose:
b. Vision Statement:
c. Mission Statement:

3. Anticipated Project Impact on Community:

4. Actual Project Impact on Community based on feedback from student developed
questionnaires and/or surveys:

5. Parental Involvement: ☐Yes or ☐No
If yes, give examples of involvement

6.  Explain how you felt during the accomplishment of your project goals and once
    your project was completed.

7.  How will your accomplishments during this project serve you or others in the
    future?

8. Explain failed attempts during this project.  What did you learn from the failed
attempts?
9. Complete a project success analysis for the community service project.

10. Can other students replicate this project by using your planning
    and procedure notebook as a guide? ☐Yes or ☐No

Experience Reflection:

# FIP-2004 Sample Item #3

The *Project Symposium Participant* Survey is a method of allowing participants to grade the presented projects during the symposium sessions. Participant feedback results from this survey, provides valued information used to "tailor" the following school year's projects. The instrument's design measures participant's perception of a member's ability to accomplish the established *Community Service-Based Project Criteria.*

Read Instructions to Participants before the Presentations Begin. Form 2: Please take the time to carefully read and complete each statement on this form. The 1-5 response scale used for each statement has the assigned point value as: 5 = Strongly Agree, 4 = Agree, 3 = Neither Agree or Disagree, 2 = Disagree, or 1 = Strongly Disagree. Using only one number per statement, signify your determined value for each statement by placing a check in the appropriate numbered column.

Be sure to ask participants to check the appropriate line to signify member or non-member participant.

# Sample Form 2: Project Symposium Participant Survey

| School Letter Head | | | | | | |
|---|---|---|---|---|---|---|
| Project Symposium Participant Survey | | | | | | |
| 1-5 response scale:  **5** = Strongly Agree  **4** = Agree  **3** = Neither Agree or Disagree  **2** = Disagree  **1** = Strongly Disagree | | | | | | |
| | Please Respond to each of the 10 Statements | 5 | 4 | 3 | 2 | 1 |
| 1. | I feel that this project reflected the vision and mission statement as presented. | ☐ | ☐ | ☐ | ☐ | ☐ |
| 2. | I feel that the displayed posters and brochures were adequate advertisement for this project. | ☐ | ☐ | ☐ | ☐ | ☐ |
| 3. | I feel that this project contributed to the community. | ☐ | ☐ | ☐ | ☐ | ☐ |
| 4. | I feel that the project notebook will not provide assistance for future members. | ☐ | ☐ | ☐ | ☐ | ☐ |
| 5. | I feel that the presenter provided insight into the planning that went into this project. | ☐ | ☐ | ☐ | ☐ | ☐ |
| 6. | I feel that the presenter adequately reflected his/her learning experiences through the completion of this project. | ☐ | ☐ | ☐ | ☐ | ☐ |
| 7. | I feel that little planning was necessary to complete this project. | ☐ | ☐ | ☐ | ☐ | ☐ |
| 8. | I feel that the presenter expressed important life long lessons that resulted from planning and implementing this project. | ☐ | ☐ | ☐ | ☐ | ☐ |
| 9. | I feel that the presenter was excited about the project during the presentation. | ☐ | ☐ | ☐ | ☐ | ☐ |
| 10. | I feel that project data added substance to the presentation. | ☐ | ☐ | ☐ | ☐ | ☐ |
| | ☐ Non-Member Participant        ☐ Member Participant | | | | | |

# FIP-2004 Sample Item #4

| Recommended Model of Excellence: Incremental Training Schedule | | |
|---|---|---|
| **Student Leadership Development**<br>[Educational Transfer] | | |
| Training: Level 1 | | Month (s) |
| a. | Measured each quarter | 10,12,3,5 |
| b. | Semester grades in core subjects | 12,5 |
| c. | TAKS results | 5 |
| d. | State and/or National Conference Presentations | As available |
| **Special Project**<br>[Student Responsibility] | | |
| Training: Level 2 | | Month (s) |
| a. | 12 Attributes of Students Gifted and Talented in Leadership (Stages I-IV) | *10,12,3,5 |
| b. | Board of Director Measurement [Project Proposals] | Begins after new year |
| c. | 2005 Project Symposium | 4 |
| **Self-Directed Learners**<br>[Self-Efficacy, Self-Regulation, and Intrinsic Motivation] | | |
| Training: Level 3 | | Month (s) |
| a. | Self Assessment | 10,12,3,5 |
| b. | Peer/Observer Assessment | 10,12,3,5 |
| c. | Coordinator Assessment | 10,12,3,5 |
| **Academic Accountability**<br> [Student Assessment Types] | | |
| Training: Level 4 | | Month (s) |
| Semester Grades | Leadership in Action | Quizzes |
| Notebook Portfolio | Project Symposium Scores | Mentor Program |
| Electronic Portfolio | SAT/ACT Scores | Protégé Program |
| TAKS Performance Commendable Rankings | Advanced Placement Courses | Pre-Advanced Placement Courses |

# Chapter 12 – Perceptual Changes

**Future Leaders**

$E_A^{L.}$ Once everything for the newly designed C. E. Ellison High School Leadership Academy was in place, I felt prepared to take on the task of attempting to change some of the less supportive teacher's misconceptions about the program. I brainstormed with my students about ideas that could help accomplish this goal. Our first effort to influence the entire internal school environment occurred on September 11, 2003. Rachel MacNealy, as a sophomore member, brought in a sample card that included our vision statement (Ellison Academy Growing Leaders of Excellence) with a yellow ribbon and small gold safety pin attached so that each teacher, administrator, and staff member could wear it on 9/11. We also made a large-scale flag that included white stars attached to a blue background and white stripes attached to a red background. Everyone at C. E. Ellison High School was welcome to sign it or write positive notes on the white portions of the flag. This group activity was in remembrance of an event that changed the United States forever.

Before the beginning of classes on the morning of 9/11/2003, we hung the large flag in the commons area. Members modeled the expected behavior of writing a positive note on the white portions and then they had their pictures taken for on lookers. We invited everyone passing by to come over and write a positive note on the flag. The flag had our new logo along with the statement, "sponsored by C. E. Ellison High School Leadership Academy" strategically placed on the flag. We took pictures and thanked everyone for their contributions. Soon there were crowds of students, teachers, custodians, and others in formed lines as they waited for their opportunity to sign the flag. That single event marked the start of changes in attitudes toward the C. E. Ellison High School Leadership Academy organization as a whole.

Though it was a simple act, it allowed all participants to feel pride as they recognized their friends and family members deployed to Iraq. The flag with all of the signatures and positive statements symbolized our ability as an organization to have an effect our internal environment. During after action reviews and various reflection activities, some of the members stated that they thought that the activity was a good one. Other members agreed, but they stated that they had never anticipated that something so simple would have made such a big difference all over the school. We took the flag down one week later, and it hang in the C. E. Ellison High School Leadership Academy classroom for the remainder of the year. The flag was a constant reminder to current members and for those who followed how that single event had marked our first successful project as an organization. At the end of the year, we rolled up the flag and stored it above the ceiling tiles. Recognition of individual's selfless contributions in response to the 9/11 events also established our first C. E. Ellison High School Leadership Academy tradition. This became a tradition and a story that current members told to the new members.

Would this single event have the power to change the perception of the teachers that I have been discussing? I would have to say, no. Some of these types of individuals seem to be their happiest when they are able to have an endless supply of topic to share and find fault with during discussions with their negative counterparts. One thing that had began to notice though, was individuals who traditionally made negative comments about the C. E. Ellison High School Leadership Academy did it much more quietly. Why, was that? Because those individuals realized they were of a minority population within C. E. Ellison High School. The majority population of teachers, staff, custodians, administrators, students (members and nonmembers) were voicing positive comments about the C. E. Ellison High School Leadership Academy. The eagerly discussed all that organization was accomplishing for its members, Killeen community, and total school environment. The perceptual change resulted in an increase in membership for the 2004-2005 school year.

## Two-Step Formula

I believe that if something is worthwhile I may initially have to sweat blood, but the rewards of such actions are priceless. Rewards were plentiful while serving as the C. E. Ellison High School Leadership Academy's Coordinator. What rewards? Rewards received through observations of students' growth in leadership development. First, experiences caused these students to believe in the willingness of others to assist them as they made their dreams become reality. Next, these students began to believe that they had the right to "dream big dreams". Then they began to develop a belief in the concept of being responsible for serving as positive role models for other students within the school and in the real world. Finally, they learned how to make use of their internal abilities and power stretching them well beyond their normal comfort zones through *Leadership in Action*.

A combination of these rewards provided a gauge the amount of guidance, support, and assistance needed by these students as they made their dreams become reality. Teaching these students that successful achievement of one's goals often takes him/her along winding and sometimes difficult paths, guided them as they began to utilize their problem-solving and critical thinking skills. By observing these students as they overcame obstacles in the path of their goals, using the ME and FIP-2004, resulted in developing the *Two-Step Formula*. The *Two-Step Formula* ensures effective student leadership development, training, and preparation.

Additionally, the formula promotes student's willingness to serve as society's future and ethical decision makers.

Two-Step Formula

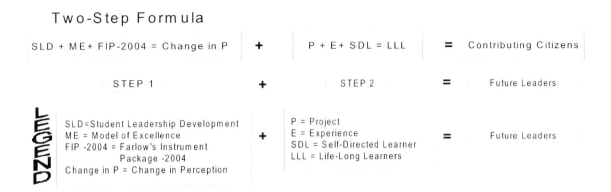

Using the *Two-Step Formula*, in turn, addresses a specific emphasis on the value of learning towards a student's ability to accomplish goals now and in the future. The effective and total implementation of the *Two-Step Formula* into public school systems will allow educational leaders further develop their own leadership skills, promote this formula for learning to their faculty and staff, so that all can share in what I have already witnessed and experienced. That is, *I have witnessed the power of belief, student's perceptual change toward becoming receptive to a quality education, and an awareness that promotes and empowers students to perform at their best.* These students strive to be the brightest, most talented, and most educated through their own actions and choices. Problem identification is one of the simplest acts to perform taking little or no additional thought process in the grand scheme solving problems. True leaders not only have the ability to identify the problem, but they are willing to take action and develop viable solutions to resolve the problem. True leaders are problem solvers to completion. This is what my students are capable of doing. Imagine a nation full of students and adults with this type of mindset and goals. Just imagine it.

## Power of Hope

I received permission to use my student leadership ideas and tools (ME and FIP-2004) as I trained the members of the C. E. Ellison High School Leadership Academy. This freedom allowed a closer look into the accomplishments of the students within the program. I began to implement my ideas and use these tools having the goal of developing the student's leadership skills. The overall process provided insight about what high school students are capable of accomplishing with the proper guidance, support, assistance, and true empowerment. The idea of empowerment truly exists only when the leader is confident enough to loosen his/her reigns, allow mistakes to be made, assist or make limited suggestions as to how to overcome the problem, and the leader is patient while the problem is being worked out by someone else. When a leader gives too much assistance, leadership growth and development of others will not really occur. These individuals are simply serving an extension of the leader. In this type of environment, innovation is rare. Allowing students certain freedoms and time for reflection about what they had experienced taught them how to modify their behavior to embrace desired goals. Having opportunities to practice and refine the skills of self-regulation to accomplish stated goals lead these students to experience an elevation in self-efficacy. These students had became equipped with the tools needed to reach the motivating factors that would drive them to accomplish specific goals or become risk takers in novice situations.

Members of the C. E. Ellison High School Leadership Academy came from a variety of backgrounds. While it is an important factor to be knowledgeable of the background or situation of students, it is equally important that he/she learns and develops an important belief. This is the belief system that guides an individual to believe that in spite of his/her environmental challenges the ability to accomplish great things for self and others is always present. As long as a "just give up" mentality is not prevail over the individual to a level of consumption. When the proper guidance, support, assistance is present this belief system becomes a real possibility and a realistic goal for the individual.

As an educator, I have shared some of my early childhood experiences with my students. This sharing is not to evoke pity or sorrow. I simply share these stories with my students to give them hope. Through the early awareness of conscious decisions, choices, and knowledge about consequences for actions taken, I became equipped to experience success in spite of environmental challenges. During times of difficulty, I learned how to call on my inner strength and power to create positive circumstances within my environment. I am not unique many other individuals possess these same abilities. Awareness simply brings them to light.

Redesigning the C. E. Ellison High School Leadership Academy into an organization that would provide students with unique experiences gave these students the inspiration to ensure that their visions became reality. At the same time, these same students had opportunities, experiences, and detailed examples of how to achieve academic success across content areas. My overall goal for redesigning the C. E. Ellison High School Leadership Academy organization was to develop students as leaders, give them opportunities to practice their learned skills through community service based projects, and enhance a transfer of knowledge that would strengthen their self-efficacy, self-regulation, and intrinsic motivation to learn. I believe that when students develop these three variables (self-efficacy, self-regulation, and intrinsic motivation to learn) they become self-directed learners

116

striving to achieve excellence. Just imagine the powerful effects of students developing this overall goal. Later in this chapter, there are a few examples of students having achieved this overall goal. Burns stated (1978) that power and leadership are measured by the degree of production of intended effects. Nationally, there is a desperate need for the development of leaders sharpened with effective knowledge and skills before entering into colleges, universities, or the work force.

## C. E. Ellison High School Leadership Academy Ambassadors

C. E. Ellison High School counselors believed in the vision of providing unique opportunities to the C. E. Ellison High School Leadership Academy members. As a result, the counselors began to provide information about national leadership conferences as they received it. Discussions took place about the possibility of sending our members to national leadership conferences. After those discussions, and checks of the budget, everyone (Mr. Rainwater, parents, members of the Board of Directors, and the coordinator) decided that the conferences would provide unique learning experiences for the members. Members of the 2003-2004 C. E. Ellison High School Leadership Academy were selected to attend the national conferences based on their particular areas of interest, good standing, and their ability to respond to the following prompt: "Why I should be selected to represent C. E. Ellison High School as a C. E. Ellison High School Leadership Academy Ambassador."

I explained the need for members to realize that this was their opportunity to sell themselves as prospective national leadership conference ambassadors. My students and I came up with the idea to use the term ambassador because of the duration of the conferences and the fact that the selected members would be representing our organization. For the first time, the C. E. Ellison High School Leadership Academy would be sponsoring member attendance at national leadership conferences. Additionally, each member was required to send a postcard during his/her conference, so that other members could read about their experiences while they were occurring. Students designed a board with a United States map entitled, *Where in the nation are lead member*s? Our historian, Roxanne Bennett a sophomore member, supplied a photograph for each member. A photograph, a string, and a pin identified and stretched across each member's state location. Two members wrote a song similar to the one used as Matt Lauer (Today Show) travels around the world. An example of the first C. E. Ellison High School Leadership Academy member to attend a national conference follows:

## Lenna Black

Lenna Black, age 17, and her post-secondary interest is law. Lenna was a very dedicated and focused member. Her personal leadership development provided her with the tools that she needed to complete high school an entire semester early. While still attending high school, Lenna completed a college course at a local junior college. She was the first member in the history of C. E. Ellison High School to complete early graduation in conjunction with having completed all of the requirements to graduate under the Distinguished Academic Program (DAP). I remember hearing a comment that Lenna had made one day during the Principles of Leadership class, she stated, "Before becoming a member of the Leadership Academy, I just wanted to be a ghost to blend in at school."

After returning from the National Youth Leadership Conference Forum on Law, Lenna made presentations about her experience to members of the Killeen Evening Rotary Club and at the 2004 Project Symposium. The following information is a summarized version of comments that Lenna made after returning from the National Youth Leadership Conference Forum on Law held in Washington D.C. She stated, "At first, I was afraid that my education would not measure up to that of the other students attending the national conference. Some of the students that would be attending the conference would be from very well off families and probably had more educational opportunities than I had had. I decided that I would make note cards about different case laws, so that I would not seem like some country Texan. I thought that I wanted to become a lawyer one day, now I know that I want to become a lawyer. I serves as an Assistant Supreme Court Judge in a mock trial!" During Lenna's leadership conference, she met and appeared in a photograph with Chet Edwards that located on his photo gallery website. She also had the opportunity to meet with John Carter while in Washington.

# Chapter 13 – Personal Experiences

## Tomorrow's Leaders

**ELA.** While continuing to read this section, try to imagine how all students might be able to transfer learning from one area (community service based projects) to other content areas and experience greater academic achievement and success. Try to imagine, students who are capable of achieving educational ownership. Try to imagine students who realize the power of their own ability to achieve greatness, the ability to regulate their own behavior, and who become intrinsically motivated due to their ability to make a difference in their environment. Still yet, try to imagine students who are self-directed learners. What comes into view? For those who can see through my eyes, it is a visual image of society's future leaders. The definition of leadership that I developed resulted from a culmination of life long experiences, an ability make unbiased observations, and the ability to identify a set of specific leadership attributes that my students exhibited as they completed their community service-based projects. *Leadership is the process of developing the power to visualize future environments, a willingness to take part in planning, individual growth, and implementing necessary resources to make visions become reality.* Giving life to this definition was an effective method utilized to provide guidance and assistance to these students as they learned the process of making their dreams become reality.

Research involving human participants proceed with great caution and seek to protect the identity of its participants. All members who provided comments in this section did so voluntarily and with written parental permission. The reason for including student's information, comments, and experiences is in the hope that their stories will generate scholarship or unique mentoring opportunities by readers in their stated areas of interest. The ages and interests of the members are as of 2004-2005.

# C. E. Ellison High School Leadership Academy Members
## 2003-2004

# Edward Huncherick, Alumni & Mentor

Age: 18

Currently: Central Texas College Freshman in Killeen, Texas

My first year as a member of the C.E. Ellison High School Leadership Academy was during the 2003 – 2004 school year. I did not know that the information and the opportunities that I experienced during that year would help change my life. My experiences within the C.E. Ellison High School Leadership Academy include the following:

- ❖ Completing the Tarleton State University in Central Texas leadership focused college course;
- ❖ Completing a community service based project (B.A.E.H. Youth Leadership Conference and B.A.E.H. Scholarship Fund);
- ❖ Presenting my project at the National Association of African American Studies and again at the Texas Association for the Gifted and Talented;
- ❖ Serving as a mentor for other members as they were in the process of completing their community service based projects
- ❖ Opportunity to receive one of the first C.E. Ellison High School Leadership Academy college scholarships;
- ❖ Taking the Principles of Leadership course

I learned many different leadership theories and values that would affect my life and the lives around me. I was only required to take the first semester of the class however; I chose to take it the full year so that I could finish the final steps of completing my project. I also served as a teacher assistant and mentored the other members during the second semester. My experiences within the C.E. Ellison High School Leadership Academy were awesome and the experiences helped me develop my own leadership skills needed to accomplish my future goals. C.E. Ellison High School Leadership Academy sponsored a three credit hour college course taught by two college Tarleton State University professors. In this course, we learned leadership theories on an individual leadership scale. We also found out our strong points and our week points. This helped me as I worked to complete my project. I knew what my week points were and I knew when it was time to ask for help. The class also helped us choose our projects, figure out who are stakeholders were, and whom we were really doing our projects for. Through this class, we also received three college credits and an official transcript. Overall, the college class helped prepare me for my project and my future.

A community-based project is a major requirement to graduate with the C.E. Ellison High School Leadership Academy. I completed two projects in one: 2004 B.A.E.H. Youth Leadership Conference and the B.A.E.H. Leadership Academy

Scholarship Fund. My partner and I used the initials of our first and last names, Brandon Antal and Edward Huncherick, to make the acronym B.A.E.H. The 2004 B.A.E.H. Youth Leadership Conference was a big project within its self. I started the project in October 2003. The scheduled date for the conference was January 31, 2004. I spent many Principles of Leadership class periods and Saturdays working on the conference. I first had to find speakers and support.

I typed a letter that needed approval on two different levels, the coordinator of the leadership academy and the principle of C.E. Ellison High School. I made several changes, several times before it received approval and sent out. After I sent the letter out to possible speakers, I then focused on writing letters to different schools to get student participation in the conference as well. I visited many local schools to talk about the conference. I also made a detailed color brochure to send with the letters so the potential speakers and the schools to advertise for the conference. There were 10 speakers and approximately 100 students attended the conference. As part of the project criteria, I made a survey for participants to fill out. This gave provided feedback about the effectiveness of the conference.

The second project was the B.A.E.H. Leadership Academy Scholarship Fund. I wanted to help graduating senior members with the cost of attending college, so the scholarship was established. An equal division of the B.A.E.H. Leadership Academy Scholarship Fund for eligible members and on the guidelines that I established as follow:

1. Eligibility Criteria:
2. Application Process,
3. Interview Process, and
4. Leadership Academy standards, guidelines, and requirements completed.

Out of eight senior members, only three members that took full advantage of the B.A.E.H. Leadership Academy Scholarship Fund and received scholarships. Senior members not applying for the scholarship funds were either planning to join the military service, received full tuition military scholarships for college, or received full academic college scholarships. These members wanted to increase the scholarship fund for members who would have a greater need. The 2004 B.A.E.H. Youth Leadership Conference and B.A.E.H. Leadership Academy Scholarship Fund projects stretched me mentally and stretched my leadership skills.

Through our coordinator, me and a few other students got the opportunity to present our projects at the TAGT conference in Houston and the National African American Studies conference in Austin. At these conferences, we stayed two days and had the opportunity to hear about other people's studies and accomplishments. We all presented our projects after our coordinator, Mrs. Farlow, gave her research presentation. We presented to many successful researchers, educators, and business people from all over the United States, China, and Africa. This opportunity helped me work on my public speaking, the way I presented my accomplishments, and myself as a whole. I do not believe I would of received this opportunity if I was not an active member of the C.E. Ellison High School Leadership Academy.

The last thing I did before I graduated in 2004 was to serve as a mentor and role model for members completing their projects from February through May. I offered my knowledge and experience to help make other student projects as successful as they wanted it to be.  In conclusion, I have grown in leadership, because of the opportunities that I experienced. I also have grown through the experience of completing my projects.  I was stretched and required to achieve at another level of leadership and another level of responsibility for myself and for others. I enjoyed my experience as a member of the C.E. Ellison High School Leadership Academy.  It was hard work but we also had a lot of fun doing each project. The things learned through the academy were not just learned, but I was also forced to use the things that I learned. The leadership skills I learned through the things I have accomplished have already changed my views on many things and they have continued to change me day by day. I am a firm believer that as long as I apply what I have learned and continue to stretch my abilities it will change my future.  I am now an alumnus of the program and I look forward to assisting the members who will take over my project during the 2004-2005 school year.

# Salwa Yordi, Alumni & Mentor

Age: 18
Currently: Central Texas College Freshman in Killeen, Texas
Area of Interest: Public Relations & Television Broadcasting

When you are originate from one country and then move to a different country, your life changes in many ways. That was exactly my case. My name is Salwa Yordi and I am from Venezuela. I moved to the United States three years ago and I attended high school at C. E. Ellison High School in Killeen, Texas without knowing how to speak English. After finishing my junior year, I joined the C. E. Ellison High School Leadership Academy. This is the only organization at our school where the opportunities that were provided to me were the best of the best.

When I first joined and enrolled in the Leadership Academy class with Mrs. Farlow as the sponsor, I saw that the academy had the purpose of helping our student body and our community at the same time. The Leadership Academy of Ellison High School teaches you how to become a better leader with a positive attitude. I learned so many fantastic things and I will never forget how some of them changed my life in a positive way. The Academy thought me how important the values of any organization are, how to do better teamwork, how to become a leader, how to fight for what you believe in, how to dream without limits, and many other great things that changed not only my life, but many others too.

The Leadership Academy completed many great projects that helped our community in so many aspects; we showed that the students are capable of affecting our community in ways that nobody could imagine. Personally, I had the opportunity of creating a project called the *Cultural Exchange*, which had the purpose of helping International students to adapt to the American culture better. Through this project, I worked with two different high schools and one middle school and this was an unforgettable experience.

My 2003-2004 high school year was amazing the Leadership Academy provided so many opportunities to its members. I had the opportunity of presenting my project at the National Association of African American Studies conference. At this conference, I met people from different cultures and that was great. The Leadership Academy did so many things for me that made me the better leader that I am today. I know that we are the future leaders and with organizations like the Leadership Academy, we can make a difference in our community. I am now a college student and I see myself as a better leader. I am growing everyday to become a leader who is willing to help anyone who needs my help.

# Hye Ji Na, Alumni

Age: 16
2004-2005 School Year: High School Junior and College Freshman
Area of Interest: Psychology/Psychiatrist

I honestly believe that my acceptance into Leadership Academy was of a divine nature; all forces, natural and supernatural, were in cahoots trying to dissipate the opportunity of me getting into this most beneficial organization. The initial moment I heard of Leadership Academy, I knew it was a unique organization that would dissolve my leadership inhibitions and allow me to be more in tune with my self-awareness, and not to mention it would look excellent on my college application. I, in my neatest handwriting, completed the application, turned it in on time, and was now just waiting for an interview. Unfortunately, the week that interviews were scheduled we encountered horrible weather and I absent from school for 2 or 3 days. My interviewer, Mrs. Farlow, called during one of the bad weather days to reschedule my interview appointment. When the weather finally cleared up and we were allowed to attend school, I was handed bad information. I was in Geometry class talking to other students about Leadership Academy when someone told me the reason they didn't apply. They said that you had to take the Leadership class all years of your high school career. I didn't have time for that! I wasn't going to waste precious space for college classes for a class that I was going to take thrice! Forget that! As luck would have it, my memory failed me and I missed my Leadership Academy interview. I wasn't too upset. Mrs. Farlow on the other hand wasn't too happy. She called me once more and after explaining myself she gave me a second chance even after concluding all interviews. I was notified of my acceptance a couple days later.

To my relief, I only had to take the Principles of Leadership course once. This class turned out to be more difficult than I first perceived. We actually worked. I came into that class knowing little about leadership but when I came out I had a major paradigm-shift. I extended my knowledge on different perspectives of leadership, the different types of leaders, the power of the Pygmalion Effect, and the reasoning behind synergy. I worked extensively with technology, which prepared me for the working field. This course was grooming future highly effective, marketable business leaders! In this class, we were also mandated to complete high-class resumes and an electronic portfolio. I would have never anticipated that as a high school student I would be compiling an electronic portfolio already. I mean adults do that, not high school students. These 2 assignments unclouded my eyes. It boosted my self-confidence because I knew that I was prepared for the "real world". It showed me how much I really accomplished, especially through the Leadership

Academy. I experienced unique opportunities that most adults don't even get a chance to experience.

It is a requirement for all members who desire to graduate with Leadership Academy distinctions to have completed a Project. A Project entails putting your passion into action or doing something beneficial for a group of people. My Project was attending a People to People Leadership Summit in California and establishing point of contacts and relaying important and useful information to Leadership Academy so they can employ it. A lot of preparation goes into a Project. I had to assemble a PowerPoint presentation and make a Project binder.

The People to People Leadership Summit was an all paid for trip by Leadership Academy. It was a very memorable experience and I would have never ever gotten this sort of opportunity had it not been for Leadership Academy. Throughout the duration of the 10-day Summit, I realized the significance of growth I received from Leadership Academy. At the end of the Summit, I know my mind was enlightened and broadened. Lifelong friendships were created that never would have been if I never heard of Leadership Academy. By "developing ambassadorial behavior and citizenship, participating in all activities, completing all academic assignments, and conceiving an action plan", I received high school credit for the Perspectives on Leadership course. I was so moved by the power of this program that I nominated Mrs. Farlow as a Group Leader because I knew she would do an exceptional job. I believe Leadership Academy will influence People to People positively in numerous ways and vice versa.

Another wonderful opportunity I experienced because of Leadership Academy's established relationships was RYLA (Rotary Youth Leadership Award) Camp. At this summer camp, I became exposed to different behavioral qualities of various leader types. We had special competitions building sportsmanship and allowing us to exemplify teamwork with our groups. We had group meetings where we bonded and expressed to each other how we felt about certain things. By the end of this camp, I appreciated the fact that there are both positive and negative leaders to learn.

Not only did I get a chance to participate in 2 exciting summer programs, I also spoke at national conferences. The NAAAS (National Association of African American Studies) Conference in Houston was the first one I attended. Mrs. Farlow decided to substantiate her leadership research with actual real-life data: her students! I was quite nervous. The thought of 20 pairs of adult eyes and ears scrutinizing my every gesture and word didn't seem like a comfortable environment. Nevertheless, I was up there, presented my project, and felt quite complacent afterwards.

I didn't realize the extent of the power Leadership Academy members held until I presented at the TAGT (Texas Association for the Gifted and Talented) Conference in Austin. I felt more at ease presenting because I had done this routine already before. After Mrs. Farlow and all the students she brought along concluded their presentations, all you could hear were the clapping of the room showering us with standing ovations. As a woman in the crowd yelled, "You guys rock!" I had an epiphany: all the achievements of Leadership Academy surmounted what most adults have accomplished. I didn't observe this because I was surrounded by it daily. However, when I stepped out of my eyes and into the mindset of a bystander, I saw how fantastic and mind-blowing it seemed that a couple of students who were empowered with ambition and vision could achieve so much. It still amazes me today. Leadership Academy's vision is to "grow leader of excellence." Mission accomplished.

During my sophomore year and second year of being part of Leadership Academy, I decided to apply to TAMS (Texas Academy of Math and Science). TAMS is a program where you can simultaneously complete your last two years of high school while you begin your freshman and sophomore year in college at the University of North Texas. Therefore, when I graduate from high school, I will be a junior in college. I thought this was an excellent way to enhance my education while getting ahead and cutting down college tuition costs. However, by applying to TAMS, I would have to accept leaving behind Leadership Academy physically. I say physically because the values that I learned from Leadership Academy will never be left behind. On the contrary, they will be applied everyday in this new and unfamiliar territory.

Since I have been accepted into TAMS, I have relinquished my Leadership Academy membership and am now considered an alumnus. Even though Fall of 2004 is the marking of my official acceptance into the TAMS institution, it does not mean that I will forget and leave behind all the invaluable lessons Leadership Academy has instilled in me for the past 2 years. It will however, certainly be a period where I can truly apply that wisdom to my studies, new relationships, and daily life. Affiliating yourself with Leadership Academy is not just a way to enrich your college application; this organization enriches you!

# Bethany Snyder

Age: 17
2004-2005 School Year: Senior
Area of Interest: Elementary Education

My name is Bethany and I am currently a senior class of two thousand and five, graduate of Ellison High School in Killeen Texas. Throughout my high school career I have been involved in various clubs and organizations, such as band, Leadership Academy, Fellowship of Christian athletes (FCA), and my church youth group.

I have been in band for the past seven years. I haven been involved in the C.E. Ellison high school Marching band for the past four years. During my freshman year, I auditioned for region band, and I ranked 7th out of the 22 people that were selected to audition. This was a major accomplishment for me. My sophomore and junior years, I played a solo for a local solo and ensemble contest, and received a one that is the highest possible rating. For the past two years, I have held the lieutenant position. As a lieutenant, I am responsible for teaching the upcoming freshman and new members our style of marching and anything else that is necessary for them to know so that our marching season is successful.

An additional organization that I joined this year is Fellowship of Christian Athletes. It's an organization where students come together on Wednesday nights for fellowship and Bible study. It's a great experience to come together with my fellow students and worship. We have the goal of positively influencing students in our school. Another organization I have been greatly involved in since my sophomore year is the leadership academy; the only one in the Killeen ISD. As a member of the Leadership Academy, I have completed at least one hundred and fifty community service hours (fifty annual community service hours) and a senior project, "The David Lubar Author's Visit". What this author visit entailed for me as a project co-coordinator were the following:

❖ Planned and organized details of an author's visit for the sophomore students at C. E. Ellison High School;
❖ Designed, printed, and distributed brochures;
❖ Development of a PowerPoint presentation;
❖ Book distribution to participating teachers and their students at C. E. Ellison High School;
❖ Making posters to advertise the project;
❖ Planned and scheduled session times for each class; and
❖ Made project presentations to counselors and sophomore classes trying to get participants for our project.

The David Lubar Author's Visit project was co-sponsored by the C. E. Ellison High School and the Leadership Academy. We determined how many students would come to each session and we provided lunch for all participating Leadership Academy members and invited guest. This project was a very long, and frustrating process, but we received a great amount of positive feedback from our surveys, so it made the whole experience worthwhile. I think it also helped me with my organization, and time management skills.

Participants in the author's visit read David Lubar's book titled, *Hidden Talents,* and we held meetings to discuss the book before the actual author visit. As participants, students met the author Mr. David Lubar, discussed his book, his writing strategies, and he signed each student's book. This project was intended to help students with the writing part of the TAKS test. This visit proved to be very effective because our school received very high scores on TAKS. Also another requirement if the leadership academy is to be a mentor, which I am now doing, I am also serving as a teacher's assistant, to the leadership academy coordinator, so help make the Leadership Academy more effective.

One of my most cherished extra curricular activities is my church youth group. I have been a member of First Baptist Church for 17 years, and have been actively involved in my youth group for six years. Every Christmas since my seventh grade year, I have been involved in project called Operation Magi. Operation Magi is where we adopt around fifteen families, and we are given information about their family, their needs, and then take money donated by members in the church and go to a local department store and buy clothes and toys for the needy family. Then wrap the presents and deliver them to the families. This has always been a great experience for me to see the look on the families face, and on the faces of their children, knowing we made a difference in someone's life.

Another project I did with my church was our summer mission trip to Arlington Texas in the summer of 2003. We went to Arlington Texas for a week and held "backyard bible studies" for children in the backyards of bad neighborhoods. There were about 15 students and over a hundred children, so we were greatly out numbered, but that only made the experience better to be able to interact with that many more children. We had story time, which was a short bible story, craft time, recreation, snack, and music time. It was an amazing experience for me not only to be able to minister to little children but also to get to interact with them. It taught me a great deal about myself and helped me make the decision of wanting to be an elementary school teacher after I graduate college.

Over the past year, I have been to Texas A&M University several times. The first time I visited the campus was on February 27th 2004, with the Leadership Academy
for a college visit. A Texas A&M University student gave us a tour and showed us Kyle field, all of the major sites on campus, and explained Texas A&M University's various traditions. I instantly fell in love with the campus. During the summer of 2004, I attended the EXPLORE camp from June 13-16, 2004. It was a great experience to live on campus, and have an idea of what it might be like to attend Texas A&M University. The experience also confirmed that I want to Major in Elementary Education. Working with small children is one of my biggest passions.

# Lenna Black

Age: 17
2004-2005 School Year: Senior/University of Mary Hardin-Baylor Freshman
Area of Interest: Law

My mom had this quote put on my senior book "there are two things that parents can bequest to give their children one of these is roots and the other is wings." My parents did this, and in a very similar way so did Leadership Academy. Leadership Academy instilled the one belief that is truly the American dream "I can do anything," and that breaking the mold is not always bad. I am now a high school graduate a semester early and I was the first ever to graduate early on the Distinguished Academic Plan, after I was told that it could not be done. In order to graduate early I had to take a couple of night classes at Central Texas College. I would get out of high school go home for fifteen minutes and then go to college. As anyone can imagine this was not the easiest way to go about getting school credit. I persisted and one of the things that kept me going was the constant support that I received from my government teacher. Most people aren't very interested in politics they watch it when they have to make a decision and ignore it the rest of the time. I don't I love politics its my hobby and so government was a fun class for me. My government teacher was impressed by the fact that I was young and interested in politics and asked me how I would be voting in the upcoming election. He was quite surprised when I told him that I would not be voting at all because at the time I was still sixteen. A couple of weeks later he told the class to bring in their voter registration cards for credit. When I asked him what I was supposed to do since I couldn't vote the entire class marveled at the fact that I was sixteen and I was the only one who made an A on the last test. The only reason I signed up for those classes because someone believed that I was capable of being better than I thought I could be myself. Now I am a freshman at a four-year university and while it's hard to leave everyone behind it is so cool to be ahead.

# Elizabeth Brown

Age: 17
2004-2005 School Year: Senior
Area of Interest: Business/Pre-Med

Throughout my high school career, I have been an active member in the Leadership Academy. The Academy allows students to take on leadership roles in the community and in school. In this organization, it's not about what you know; it's about your willingness to learn and putting your learning to good use. I have acquired much knowledge from every task that I have had to undergo. While in my junior year, I learned and experienced the most of what the Academy has to offer-which was mostly due to the leadership of our former adviser Mrs. Farlow.

For my community-based project, which I completed during my junior year, two fellow Academy members and I coordinated a blood drive through a local hospital. This was a very tedious project and allowed me to learn about the planning, publicity, and organization that go into such an event. The greatest thing about the project was the impact that we (three teenagers) could have on the community. Because of the blood, we collected that day; hundreds of people were helped and possibly saved by the donations of others.

In addition to the opportunity to hold a blood drive that year, I was able to earn three hours of college credit by taking a course through Tarleton State University called Business and Society. By taking this course, I was able to get a glimpse of what college classes are like and how much learning is possible through the teachings of great professors.

Because I have been a part of the Leadership Academy, my social skills have improved. Before coming to high school, I attended a private, Christian school; when I began high school, I didn't know anyone. However, because of projects and community service brought about by the Academy, I have met many people who I am proud to say that I know.

Moreover, the leadership skills that I have acquired have helped me to succeed in other areas of school. While in high school, I have been a Senator in Student Council, the Vice-President of the Travel Club for two years, Historian of the National Honor Society, Woodwind Captain in the marching band, Teacher's Assistant for the Leadership Academy, and this year, my biggest challenge thus far- a Drum Major in the band.

All of the leadership positions that I have been able to hold are due to the many things that I have learned in the Leadership Academy. The Academy not only teaches you to lead but to want to succeed in life by taking these positions to further your development as a person. I hope that next year as I go off to Texas A&M

University, I will be able to take everything that I have learned and use it to help me pursue my education and future career.

# Roxanne Bennett

Age: 16
2004-2005 School Year: Junior
Area of Interest: Digital Graphic Design & Advertising

I knew when I was in middle school that I wanted to do something great during my high school career. Options ranged from sports, to academic programs, to community service clubs. Little did I know what path was best for me. Towards the end of my freshmen year in high school, I was already involved with J.R.O.T.C., Student Council, and a program that made blankets for sick children, called Comfort for Kids. However, out of all of these clubs there was something still missing, an anchor. I was in search of an organization that would help me enhance my leadership skills by providing me with a thorough knowledge about the basic traits of a true leader. I had been tossed into action, told to act like a leader without having any proper training on the structures of a strong leader. I was intimidated and afraid that I was incompetent. I craved for a foundation.

An answer to my problems soon came, and it was more than I could have possibly hoped. The C.E. Ellison Leadership Academy soon filled the gap and helped to form a powerful drive within me. I found myself unknowingly applying what I learned in the class to my daily life. Leadership became more than just a skill to me. It became who I was and who I want to be. It became a practice for me. I am now in my junior year of high school and have experienced situations and opportunities that many college students have not had the chance to encounter. As historian of Leadership Academy, I put together the first-ever documented history of the Academy. I have attended leadership conferences where I have spoken in front of a room full of adults about the Leadership Academy. The feeling that I received while standing in front of those adults was one of both pride and astonishment. I, a 15 year-old high school student, was sharing my views in a formal conference of adults. They were intrigued and seemed to be just as amazed as I was. Mrs. Farlow, the C.E. Ellison Leadership Academy Coordinator, had believed in the abilities of her student's so much that she had trusted us to speak at this conference.

As my teacher, she has helped me to realize that the power to stand out as a leader is within all people. I then embraced that inward ability and exerted it in my daily life. Other opportunities that came to me included the following:

- ❖ A trip to the state capital where I learned how bills are passed,
- ❖ A trip to Texas A&M University to explore the possibility of attending that college in my future, and
- ❖ A trip to a Youth Leadership Conference in Austin where I had the chance to hear speakers from various backgrounds and so much more!

Leadership is a continuous learning process. I fail at tasks, as do most people, but I am determined not to give up. As part of my growth process, I plan to present my project to local middle schools in an attempt to fill others in about the leader in all of us. I hope to have others realize that some dreams can become reality, as I have.          Another plan for my future includes attending one of the out-of-state trips that is provided to eligible and interested members. Students can attend one of several different youth summits to learn about law, medicine, leadership and more. I am also constructing a project with a fellow Leadership Academy member. We are coordinating a youth leadership camp. It will be a three-day camp and will take place at a resort nearby. Students from our local middle schools will be invited to attend. Our mission is to empower future leaders to embrace their inner leadership skills.  In all, joining the C.E. Ellison Leadership Academy is one of the greatest choices I have made in my life.  I have experienced and learned so much. It has drastically changed my life, and for that I am thankful to all of those that have helped me in my journey.

# Rachel MacNealy

Age: 16
2004-2005 School Year: Junior
Area of Interest: Medicine

At the end of my sophomore year, I made a decision that surprised many in the school. I chose to try out for the Cheerleading squad instead of continuing her successful dance activities. Why would someone so successful and at the top of her form in one field elect to give it all up for the unknown? The thought of voluntarily giving up the comfort of being the best at something and starting over in a different activity is enough to frighten most people into inaction. Instead of being paralyzed though, I seemed to thrive on the challenge. My story illustrates leadership in action.

The Emeralds Dance and Drill team has a great reputation, a great director, and they always look and perform superbly. Throughout elementary and middle school, I worked hard to reach my goal of being an "Emerald" and when I made the team as a freshman, I was ecstatic. During my first year, many of the veterans on the team encouraged me, challenged me, and provided tremendous support. They were my mentors and although I didn't realize it at the time, they provided me many lessons in leadership.

I wanted to be a leader on the team and had seen that leaders had to set high standards and be able to meet them. During my freshman year, I had the chance to begin working toward a leadership role; the dance team director offered me the opportunity to compete in a duet during a national competition. My duet partner and I had to tryout to earn the right to compete. We worked incessantly, taking private dance technique lessons, training at night, on weekends, and during holidays trying to perfect the dance. I danced sometimes until my feet bled. The effort paid off when we won the title "National Champions" at the competition.

Expectations were even higher my second year on the team. To be eligible for a leadership position as a junior, sophomores had to compete in the solo category during competition season. Again, I worked furiously, motivated by the high standards of the team and by a desire to represent my school to the best of my ability. Again, I was fortunate when it came to competition season. My team won every competitive category in both a regional and a national competition and I was privileged enough to earn recognition as first runner up at the regional and third runner up at the national, competing against a field of fifty soloists.

Although I was happy for my team and proud of our collective achievements, I didn't feel contributing to my school to the best of my ability. I was searching for something more. Coincidently, during the year I began to understand some of the principles I was learning through my participation in the Leadership Academy. For example, instead of complaining about something, leaders develop a plan, take action, and become part of the solution to make it better - the only way to make a positive difference is to get involved.

I heard wonderful things about the Emeralds all my life, but I never heard much about the cheerleading squad. They seemed to be the perpetual underdogs with little support, constantly changing sponsors, a high turnover rate, and were having a tough time. The Emeralds were winners before I became a member and I knew they would continue to be a strong team, with or without me. As the year progressed, I realized I wanted to put into practice the many things I was learning in the Leadership Academy and the Principles of Leadership class to help another organization in our school, with the goal of getting more students actively involved in school activities. The right place seemed to be the Cheerleading Squad.

I've heard my parents occasionally say that it's good to come out of the 'comfort zone' occasionally. Although I felt comfortable as a dancer, I decided to give up my personal comfort to contribute what I could to help boost school spirit as a cheerleader. It was a hard choice to leave the dancing, but as I learned by studying many leaders throughout history, leaders take appropriate risks.

I tried out for the cheerleading squad and made it. I was nervous about what would happen, but things have turned out great so far. For example, during our Cheerleading summer camp at Texas A&M University, our squad really worked well together and improved tremendously. Before the first week of school, we covered the campus with motivational items and when school started, many students went out of their way to make positive comments about what we had done. This was a big change from previous years and we all felt we had achieved something small, but important. We were working together toward the same goal as a team!

I have used many aspects of what I learned in the Leadership Academy to help make a positive contribution to the Cheerleading squad and as the year goes on, I'm sure we will be able to get more students to actively participate in school activities helping contribute to positive school spirit. The more experiences I have in life, the more I realize how important it is to understand how to be a leader as well as when to be a good follower. I have learned that to some extent, everything in life involves varying levels of leadership, good or bad, and I want to be a good leader to make positive changes in peoples' lives. The Leadership Academy is helping me reach that goal.

I was fortunate to be selected to represent Ellison High School at the National Student Leadership Conference (NSLC) for Health and Medicine at the University of Maryland during June of 2004. This scholarship opportunity came about as a direct result of Ellison's Leadership Academy and the confidence I gained in my own abilities through the Principles of Leadership class I took during my sophomore year.

Although I had read the informational material before I departed, I was nervous about what to expect during the eleven-day conference. I imagined it would be endless meetings and classes, but when I arrived, I discovered I was completely wrong. We did have a few classes and meetings, but they directly supported our many visits to Health and Medicine related facilities around the Washington, D.C. area. When we did meet during the conference, the faculty made the meetings interesting and entertaining.

One of the many areas that grabbed my attention was medical ethics. It made me think about all the many ethical choices health care workers face every day. I also learned about the links between public policy and law to medical ethics. For example, we discussed the complications of making decisions about who should receive donated organs or financial assistance for serious medical needs. We were placed in the position of being on a medical board, deciding who should receive financial assistance to get a potentially life saving transplant, a rock star, a newborn baby, or a medical researcher working on a cure for a terrible disease. Leaders in the medical field face very complex and emotional issues.

Another one of the interesting activities we participated in was the 'personality' test and explanation. Although I probably knew it subconsciously, I was fascinated by how much people's personalities influence personal interaction and leadership. If you know about someone's personality, it can help you deal with that person more effectively and become a better leader.

The conference enabled me to meet many wonderful people from all over the world who share my interest in Health and Medicine. Although I was intimidated when I first got to the conference, I soon realized that most of the attendees had the same goals and aspirations as I have, and they like to have fun too.

In addition to all the medical and health care information, the conference provided a lot of information about how to prepare for college. The experience helped me focus my thoughts about where I might want to go to school and gave me some insights into ways of preparing for entrance exams and the admissions process.

I probably would not have participated in the NSLC program before gaining the kind of confidence I did through the Ellison Leadership Academy and our Principles of Leadership class. Although I had participated in many community and school activities and subconsciously learned leadership techniques, the Leadership Academy helped me 'connect the dots' and recognize my leadership abilities, giving me confidence in my actions.

The NSLC was a tremendous experience, but my experiences in the Leadership Academy, ranging from a speech to a national leadership education conference in Houston, Texas; to planning, coordinating, and executing my Senior Project a year early; to organizing a 9/11 Remembrance project taught me a lot about myself. I grew from avoiding participation in-group discussions because I thought I might not have quality input to recognizing that I had the knowledge, skills, and even the obligation to contribute to the activity.

The experiences I have had as a result of the Leadership Academy allowed me to meet some great people and realize that every field of life needs good leaders who want to make a positive contribution. The program has changed me and I strongly recommend the NSLC experience and the Leadership Academy program for all students who have an interest in leadership. Additional accomplishments follow:

❖ I maintained an overall 'A' average in an advanced placement curriculum;
❖ All-district as a varsity golfer;
❖ Earned two President's Student Service Awards for volunteer work on community service projects; member of the Mayor's Task Force on Teen Pregnancy;
❖ National Honor Society;
❖ Awards and recognition for excellence as a dancer on the school's highly respected Dance Team and as a sophomore; and
❖ I was an active participant in the C. E. Ellison High School Leadership Academy.

# Yeraldin Yordi

Age: 17
2004-2005 School Year: Senior
Area of Interest: Public Relations/Business

Coming from a different country, Venezuela, three years ago was not very easy. The expectations as in school performance and enrollment in different clubs/organizations were not very high, but I guess I was wrong. After probably six months, my English was not anymore an obstacle because I did not any when I came, and I noticed that I had goals that I wanted to achieve, the opportunities were visible. Attending to a very diverse school, C.E. Ellison High School offered a variety of clubs few organizations for different interests. I was really caught by an organization in special, the Leadership Academy; my sister had enrolled to this organization before I had and by her great comments and new and better performance overall I wanted to join.

The organization has high standards that any positive leader in the community would like to enroll; I was not the exception. I joined Leadership Academy in the winter of 2003, during my junior year. I started as a teacher assistant for our coordinator Mrs. Farlow and the Leadership Academy. The experience I gained from being a teacher assistant did not only contribute to my knowledge about the Leadership Academy, but it enormously helped me develop my leadership skills and performance in general.

Anyone could say that he or she is a leader, but after going to a rigorous development through the Academy, I knew that leader was not only a word, but also more likely "action:" Action that I would later utilize in different activities that I was going to have. It was already spring of 2004, when I received an invitation from the Global Young Leaders Conference held at Washington D.C. and New York City. I presented the invitation to the coordinator Mrs. Farlow to see if there were any possibilities of me going to that trip sponsored by the Leadership Academy. Leadership Academy then sponsored me to this trip after the members of the board, founder, and coordinator approved it.

A once in a lifetime opportunity was given to me thanks to the Leadership Academy and my active participation in all the related activities, meetings, community service that I had done in less than a year. I went to the Global Young Leaders Conference (GYLC) in the summer of 2004: At this conference I knew I had gained a lot of experience that I was putting on practice, taking leadership roles and giving my sharing my knowledge with others.

I have seen seniors successfully graduate as members of the Leadership Academy, my sister, Salwa Yordi, was one of them. Now I am a senior looking forward to the great opportunities others have had thanks to the Academy and coordinator, who is always looking out for her students. I know that the Academy works as a whole and we make a great difference not only in our community, but we make a difference our own selves. We are young leaders that are being taught how to be better and how to make things better. Leadership Academy I will truly say has been the organization at C.E. Ellison High School that has given a clear vision of what leadership is.

# Jessica Nicole Black

Age: 16
2004-2005 School Year: Sophomore
Area of Interest: Physical Therapist/Researcher

It took her leaving in order for me to realize that Mrs. Farlow would inspire me to live life with integrity. A rags to riches story, a quest to teach kids how to live more effective lives, and an archetypal hero that God brought to Ellison High School. For some reason every time I think of Mrs. Farlow, a cricket comes to mind. A cricket because like Jiminy Cricket Mrs. Farlow acts as my conscience. The voice in my head telling me "NO!" when I am thinking of "letting a paper wait until Monday." She also reminds me of a Lion, always on the prowl to find ways to help her pack. She always persevered and never gave up on me, never failing to show her genuine care for my future.

I remember one day last year when I had first joined the leadership academy, I walked in the room as Mrs. Farlow was teaching about responsibility. As I patiently waited for her to finish so I could ask about the field trip to ATM, a loud "BOOM!!!" then a "CRACK" rang in my ear. A student had just dropped one of Mrs. Farlow's brand new computers. I watched the computer in what could only be explained as slow motion drop to the floor, I noticed as the whole class, with cringing faces looked at the broken computer then back up at Mrs. Farlow. Then I watched as the lion turned to rage "Now what have I been teaching on for the past twenty minutes!!!" she yelled ......Silence...followed... "Well won't someone answer me!!!" I, in a quiet and shrilled voice whispered ... "responsibility." "Responsibility?" asked Mrs. Farlow, questioning to test the girls confidence, something that she would do many times after this day. Mrs. Farlow started to lecture on just that. RESPONSIBILITY the whole class plus one listened in silence thinking about all the times we had been irresponsible, letting her down. All and all Mrs. Farlow always knew what to do in any situation and in this one she had taken the opportunity to show us that everyone makes mistakes and you must stand up and take responsibility.

# Ryan Hockenbrocht

Age: 16
2004-2005 School Year: Sophomore
Area of Interest: Elementary Education

How the EHS Leadership Academy has influenced my Life!

When I started my freshman year at Ellison High School, I was very shy, quiet and pretty much kept to myself. I am hearing impaired, so that caused me to withdraw from others, which I had been doing for many years. Since I had such trouble understanding what was being said, I hated to introduce myself to others and speaking in front of the class was a very stressful experience for me.

One of my teachers recommended that I become part of the Leadership Academy, so my parents and I talked it over, and we agreed that it would be a good idea. That recommendation started me on a path for positive self-esteem! At first, being part of this group was a little overwhelming, and I did not really know how to fit in, but between Mrs. Farlow and many of the other members, I began to let down my "wall". I began to understand that being a part of the Leadership Academy was going to be one of the best experiences of my life!

Every morning before school, I went by to check with Mrs. Farlow, our coordinator, to make sure I was on track with what everyone else understood during the meetings, that I might not have heard. She always took the time to set me straight. Having had these discussions, I went to our meetings, and had the same information all the other students had. As time went on, I still went by to visit with Mrs. Farlow just for fun, because I was feeling confident enough to ask the others in the Academy for clarification, instead of always asking her. I began to be asked to participate in the decision-making process for activities that were being done in the Academy. Throughout this process, I became more comfortable to say what was on my mind during the meetings. I even felt that if I disagreed with an idea that I could voice my opinion, and it would really matter!

Through group activities that we did, I began to realize that I had many special gifts that I could share with others. I learned what community service was, and found that it was something that I really enjoyed. I started to realize that I was in charge of my future, and I could make it what I wanted it to be. I began to think of others, before thinking of myself, and how I could help and support them in their endeavors or projects. I began to volunteer to help in many different areas of my community. I volunteered to help people complete paperwork to receive shots at the free clinic, worked at a concession stand for two of our church's activities, volunteered at a local elementary school, helped coordinate a summer reading camp at a public library, and helped box food at the Food for Families Drive.

As the school year progressed, I became increasingly involved in all aspects of the Leadership Academy. I was in charge of making sure all the freshmen in the Academy knew when and where the meetings would be held. A phone tree was made, and I would make the phone calls to communicate the necessary information. The fact that I was actually in charge of such an important job, made me feel very proud.

I do not know what my future holds in store for me, but I do know this: The EHS Leadership Academy has allowed me to grow in ways that I could never have dreamed. Beginning high school is a very difficult time for all kids, and was for me, especially with my hearing problems. Being part of the Academy made so many things, which would have been major roadblocks for me, become learning opportunities instead. I learned how to "attack" roadblocks not let them "attack" me. Life is full of roadblocks. It is how you deal with them that if you are a winner or loser. I feel like the learning I did in Leadership has begun to prepare me for "real" life. At this stage in my life, I am beginning to think seriously about my life career. Since I have done so much volunteering and working with others, I am thinking I would like to be a teacher, that way I could work with students and help them prepare for their futures.

The Leadership Academy at Ellison has helped me become the person I am today. I am confident in not only my abilities as a student, but more importantly, as an individual. Former teachers cannot believe the difference in me since I was in their classes. They ask me what made the difference in my confidence level, and I have to say, "I am part of the Ellison High School Leadership Academy". Thanks Mrs. Farlow, for helping me become my best ME!
Ryan Hockenbrocht

# Dorothy Yu Patterson

Age: 16

2004-2005 School Year: Junior

Area of Interest: Missionary in Africa

Hey Mrs. Farlow, this is my essay that I wrote...I hope you like it and I hope the people who read your book will like it too! Oh yeah...this is Dorothy, just so you know.... and thank you for the opportunity.

"I believe that every student when given the opportunity, can make a difference."(Angela Farlow, 2004) Those words are forever be buried into my heart because they mean something to me and I believe it too. I thank God that he has found a way to give me an opportunity that could make me a better person and in the end help me to make a difference.

It all started when Mrs.. Farlow invited me into the Leadership Academy. That was the start of my opportunity, and I took it. Although it has been a short amount of time getting used to the organization, overall I have learned more about what is out there in the real world. I can do more things than I have ever thought of! It is an honor to be part of the Leadership Academy.

During this short amount of time being in the Academy, I have learned a couple of things to help me have a better life. They are part of the key points to leadership. The first point I have learned about leadership is that we have to acquire a vision for our futures. My vision and my dream is that I want to be a missionary in Africa, teaching music. That is my goal. I want to help people in a poor environment understand and make music, which is my passion. I know it can happen.

The second point that I have learned is that we need to take steps to get to our goals in life. Right now, I am in the Leadership Academy. I am understanding not only about leadership, but also about life and how to make it better for myself. The Academy is preparing me for life, so that I can get the best and do the best for others and myself. College is another step for me. I want to go to Baylor University, Major in music and minor in missions or bible study. After college, I do not have the exact plan, but I know my goal is to end up in Africa, doing what I know best and what I love. It will be hard, and I know I will need to take risks, but I believe that I can make a difference.

## Dreams of Hope

The combination of the training that I was able to fully exercise provided students with the means of achieving greater success ratios in their future endeavors. My research using the ME and FIP-2004 for the identification of student leaders and for the identification of students who are gifted and talented in leadership, has proven to be successful with the students that participated in this training. These students are capable of clearly articulating their dreams for the future, but they are also willing to take the necessary actions to make their dreams become reality. Additionally, the research also provides and guidelines designed to maximize what students will *be and do* as a result of implementation of the ME and FIP-2004 components into a student leadership development program.

The idea of developing leadership programs specifically at the high school level, has still not gained the support from some administrators, teachers, or policy makers. Some of the non-supporters of academically based leadership programs view students at the secondary education level as being to young to comprehend what it means to become a leader. Why fill a student's head with a bunch of stuff that they cannot use right now? My statement to ideas of this nature that incubate inaction is, since it is widely accepted that leadership and the word *development* indicate a process, why delay preparation until individuals have entered into adulthood. The fact is that by delaying leadership development until adulthood mistakes may be costly and directly affect an individual's livelihood. The earlier these skills are learned, the more likely these skills will become a habitual way of life for students.

## Precedent Established: Will it Continue?

I had originally believed that all of 2003-2004 accomplishments within the C. E. Ellison High School Leadership Academy organization would continue even in my absence as coordinator. At least I held this belief if the students were allowed to remain active participants within the organization. The sometimes difficult journeys that we traveled together during the 2003-2004 school year has left an imprint, of what can and should be, in their minds. Some of the roads traveled to accomplish successes during the great journey were not easy, and many of students became angry with me due to my methods of holding them responsible and accountable as society's future leaders.

I eagerly observed some of my *wonderful leaders of the future* pout, whisper, and make faces when they thought I was not looking. Is anyone willing to guess what this anger created? It created responsible and accountable students. It also created students who have a realistic awareness of their internal power, who have the ability to regulate their own behaviors, and the intrinsic motivation to take ownership for their own education. These students became self-directed learners striving to achieve not only academic success, but also success in other areas of their lives. Later during the school year, we discussed and laughed about some of their most angry moments. Those reflections signaled their individual and personal growth to me.

I explained to my students that when, or if, I were to ever change to a new position of employment, that I expected them to assist the new coordinator. This was in the hope that the traditions, culture, and belief systems we had established would continue. A large part of a successful leader's duties and responsibilities is to ensure training and empowerment of his/her people, so that once the leader is gone, the organization can continue as it did while the leader was there. This is not to say that the transitions that will occur will be easy, but they are possible. Change is a normal part of life that even occurs on a cellular level on a daily basis; most people over 35 will both relate and attest to this statement. Change is inevitable. What makes change different for each individual depends on the methods employed or one's perception of how he/she should react to the changes that are taking place.

Because the graduation date for my Master of Education degree was fast approaching, I had to make a decision. This degree allowed me so serve in a principal capacity for the public school system. I felt that I needed to prepare my students for the possibility that I might be leaving the C. E. Ellison High School Leadership Academy as its coordinator. Together we had established a strong and trusting relationship, and I didn't want to leave and have them feel unprepared to continue all that we had experienced together, or as if I had abandoned them. I believed that my students were more than capable of effectively completing the task of assisting the new coordinator for another successful year. Reasoning for this belief, these students had been actively involved in all aspects and decision- making processes that had made the program such a success.

The methods of instruction used had enhanced my student's ability to make good sound decisions based on high moral and ethical character as society's future leaders. It was expected, and even sometimes demanded, and of course, they made me proud by accomplishing it. These are the true rewards of teaching. Teachers have the opportunity and power to assist in the successful development of our future society. This is a powerful statement. The innovative activities and successful accomplishments that came to exist within the C. E. Ellison High School Leadership Academy established the new precedent in 2003-2004. Successful changes and accomplishments were recognized not only by me and the C. E. Ellison High School Leadership Academy members, but these successes were also noticed by the KISD Board of Trustees, C. E. Ellison High School Leadership Academy Board of Directors, teachers, community leaders, parents, and non-member

147

students. At no other time, had the C. E. Ellison High School Leadership Academy's name been such a positive "buzz" phrase. This positive buzz was occurring both within the C. E. Ellison High School and surrounding community. I do not claim credit for all of the successes experienced within the C. E. Ellison High School Leadership Academy. The real credit for the successes was simply the result of opening the door, and allowing the members and educational stakeholders in so that they could work their magic. It did seem magical at times. I once stated, "It just seems as if everything that is touched, turns into gold."

By establishing and redesigning the goals and objectives of the program during the 2003-2004 school year, students, staff, teachers, community leaders, and administrators finally realized the purpose of the organization's existence. Misconceptions about C. E. Ellison High School Leadership Academy's elitist mentality were out of the door. The misconception and clarification was due to a realization of the capabilities and positive assets that the members of the C. E. Ellison High School Leadership Academy were contributing to the whole school environment. Recognizing these students as influencing their immediate environment was well overdue. The intent, purpose, and goals of the organization were openly exposed and expressed, relieving the suspicious nature of the program once held by many within C. E. Ellison High School. The individuals mentioned earlier, will expect similar accomplishments to be continued or an enhancement of the program during the coming years; anything less would be defined a program failure. While the C. E. Ellison High School Leadership Academy composes only approximately 4% of the total school population, these few students have had a massive impact on their surrounding environments. Just imagine the overall over all impact that felt by everyone if all high school students believed that they were capable of functioning with a high performance culture mentality. I still find myself worrying about the growth and leadership development of the students at C. E. Ellison High School and the C. E. Ellison High School Leadership Academy members. I still keep in contact with many of the parents of my former students because we were able to establish lasting friendships due to our mutual respect, support, and commonalities. We also had mutually shared goals for the development, growth, and effective preparation for the future aspirations of tomorrow's leaders (their children and my extended family).

After only a few months of leaving the C. E. Ellison High School Leadership Academy as the coordinator, I have learned of many differences in the 2004-2005 school year's focus, level of effective student leadership development, and attitudes about the ability of my former students who are capable of running the entire organization with or without a coordinator. I have that much faith in the abilities of my students. As stated earlier, before resigning on August 30, 2004, I explained to my students that they would need to give support and assistance to the new C. E. Ellison High School Leadership Academy Coordinator. I will provide an example of the confidence that these young leaders are willing to exhibit through their transformations while in the program. The three teacher's assistants (Elizabeth Brown, Bethany Snyder, and Thomas Beaumont), prepared lesson plans, began teaching *The 7 Habits of Highly Effective People* (Covey, 1989) in the Principles of Leadership course. They prepared and gave writing assignments, learning objectives, and exams to new members during their teacher's assistant periods.

Having only three Principles of Leadership classes, these students were teaching all of the classes based on what they learned the year before while taking the course. These students were fully prepared to continue this way in order to give Mr. Rainwater ample time to select the best person for the job. I also might add, only one of the students is planning to become a teacher. Talk about being outside of a comfort zone. This shows how willing these students were to perform in the organization's time of need. They each wanted to ensure that what had been gained in one year was continued through their own willingness to take on a real world initiative. Instead of receiving recognition for their selfless dedication, these students began to feel that their efforts were unappreciated (not by members) and tied hands. In a message from one student, I received the following statement,

> We are like a country without a president. I have tried keeping people's spirits up and telling them that we are going to get a new coordinator and things will get back on track soon, but everyone is saying that the Leadership Academy is not going to be as it used to be.

Reading this statement tore at my heart. Even now, as I read the statement a lump forms in the top of my throat. I believe in my former students, in their ability to utilize their effectively developed leadership skills and I would challenge their level of leadership development against any post-secondary student including many adults. Why? These students hold strong to the belief that chronological age is not a barrier for true leadership. These students believe that true leadership exhibition occurs through action not just words, pretenses, or positions. These students believe in leadership for the real world, and that action is what gives life to the definition of leadership that I have developed. *Leadership is the process of developing the power to visualize future environments, a willingness to take part in planning, individual growth, and implementing necessary resources to make visions become reality.* One evening as I watched a television show, *The Apprentice*, I tried to imagine the actions that my students would take in the various situations and scenarios. I almost contacted the network, but I decided that I would wait until after the publication of this book. I wish C. E. Ellison High School Leadership Academy program the best and many successes in the future. I extend these genuine wishes for the success of the program because I still care deeply for the student members there. These students are members of my extended family and I will keep in contact with them and provide assistance to them for as long as they want or need me to.

# Chapter 14 – New Directions

## Gains and Losses

E$_A^L$. Implementing any program for one year is not enough time if the intent is to achieve lasting change. In order to benefit from the full effects of the any newly implemented program realistically requires a minimum of three years. There are multiple benefits for devising a three-year implementation period. A few benefits are to have access to student leadership development, growth, and actions for comparisons over a specified period. This is a necessary part of any type of research in order to gauge the amount of successful program intervention. I found through my experiences at the C. E. Ellison High School Leadership Academy that regardless of how successful one year of intervention may have been, a change in personnel too soon causes a loss of accomplishment. Often, before a proven effective leader has an opportunity to build on the successes that he/she experienced during a one-year period it is time for him/her to move on.

The new individual selected by the educational leader, often having no training for the new position, tries his/her hand at success. The opportunity for continuing to build on what has already proven successful and accomplished is lost. This is largely due to differences in personality, style of performance, and the enduring understanding of the vision of the person that he/she is replacing. Organizational successes and accomplishments having groundbreaking results that have been lost due to personnel changes, is not the fault of the new individual. He/she has simply walked into a situation. The real blame for this continuing cycle of personnel changes cannot exclude the educational leader that allowed the change in the first place. Sometimes these changes occur when an educational leader fells powerless in the presence of an effective leader. Why? Because for many years, he/she could have had a single idea, based on incomplete methods and implementation, yet the idea has a long flight due to a lack of checks and balances by his/her superiors.

Educational leaders acting as puppets because they don't truly have a vision, or those who take no action because of fear to cause a ripple in "still waters" really don't have a place in today's public education facilities. This type of educational leader has usually become complacent about the public education system as a whole, about the possibility of the academic success and achievement of today's students in the public education system, and because they are "visionless". He/she is a leader who willingly sits perched atop a tree, with watchful eyes, waiting for an effective leader to come along to correct wrongs, unite others for the cause, welcoming all credit, and organizational accomplishments. Once everything is in place and going well beyond expectations, this type of leader is somewhat relieved when the time comes for a few changes to take place. Due to a lack of vision and attention to detail, the leader has developed a false belief system about change and the ease with which it can occur. This system of belief and eagerly acting upon it, often negating the efforts brought forth by the transformative leader, makes continuing the same successful processes seem possible and even perhaps an easy task. If program or organizational success is the ultimate goal, there is no need to worry about receiving a large or total division of credit for success. Team players win when the organization as a whole wins. All of the topics that I have just mentioned (acting as a puppet, becoming complacent, lack of vision, false belief system, and division of credit worry) must be overcome before the organization can accomplish and maintain success allowing the organization to move forward.

## Time Standard Establishment

I suggest a three-year minimum implementation period for student leadership training's full adoption by public school systems. The reason for this frame of time is so that students are able to reap the rewards of student leadership training and development in its entirety. What students learn today becomes a way of life for students with strengthened possibilities tomorrow. What will student leadership training accomplish in the end? The answer is to this question are students proactively engaged, committed, and taking the initiative to direct change as opposed to becoming subjected to impositions caused by other's reactions to change. This three-year minimum will allow discussions of program effectiveness and evaluations to simultaneously occur in multiple public educational environments. This time standard also allows program intervention measures and calculations to occur for student success and achievement for a specified period. Additionally, establishment of this time standard allows for effective personnel training, successful program implementation, and a sense of urgency, yet realistic goals for full program implementation.

School districts will need to establish teams of individuals selected specifically for program participation having a three-year minimum contract. This three-year minimum contract must include termination clauses for individuals failing to fully follow the standards and guidelines of the program. Teams within the participating school districts will utilize a developed network system for the program. Information dissemination and result comparisons will take place using this program's network system. Once a month, each participating school will use a website developed for the program to update data, input data, and include both student and program accomplishments. Multiple comparisons for data collection information and data analysis can take place via the website. Non-participating school districts can also have access to the Internet site. This will to give them an idea about the workings of the program and an effective method of providing opportunities of student academic achievement and success within their own school districts.

Adequate funding availability, working much like that of Advanced Placement or Pre- Advanced Placement annual training, for one main program team coordinator to continue training, receive the latest program updates, and personal interactions with each other team coordinators needs to be established annually. The location of the annual training sessions could change annually to the location of school districts participating in the program. In this way, public school tours, auditorium availability, and cafeteria facilities would all cut cost for program participation. Effective training does not have to be costly or take place in glamorous environments. Sometimes an effective method of program training needs to take place in the environment in which its use is intended, in this case, public educational facilities. The results of the three-year time standard and continued program coordinator training are ones of program uniformity and consistency.

After two full years of program implementation and intervention, consolidated evidence and information presentations for state and national policy makers takes place. At this same time, program team coordinators will determine if they wish to continue in their current positions. The two-year marker for program team coordinators leaves an entire year for replacement selections to take place if needed, and if so, newly selected individuals can receive effective leadership development training before entering into the program. The current program team coordinator will serve as a mentor for his/her own replacement personnel for a year. This method ensures that selected individuals have had time to "buy in" to the goals and objectives of the program before they are charged with the program's implementation.

The first offer for a new program team coordinator goes to the program's current team members. This will not only cut the cost of training an individual who is totally new to the program, but it also serves to set minds of students, staff, parents at ease because they already know the individual. The team member selected as the upcoming program team coordinator has already bought into the program's vision. If not, this individual should not be serving as a member of the program's team in the first place. The statement, "no child left behind" will become a reality for a much larger majority of students attending public school facilities.

## New Program Personnel Training

As with any other successful organization, the individuals charged with implementing a new program must receive proper training to in increase the guarantee for the program's success. It is imperative that these selected individuals undergo effective leadership development training. These individuals are vital to the successful implementation of a new student leadership program. In the public educational setting, training should occur during the summer months and include a stipend for the participants. Benefits of training during the summer months allow program coordinators or other team member's areas needing improvement corrections occur before beginning the new school year.

Identification and training of team players for the new program team makes everyone aware of the level of personal responsibility and individual roles during the implementation phase of the student leadership program. All identified players and their leaders should receive the same training. Training needs to focus on establishing a common set of goals, vision, and mission statement that are complimentary to those of the school, district, and state. The new program's vision and mission statements for their student leadership development program also must occur during the summer training sessions. I have found that if completed in a timely manner the benefit of information dissemination to all educational stakeholders promotes "buy-in" and program support.

Neglecting these preparations which allows the new school year to begin on a solid and unified foundation will likely result in the teachers and staff not directly involved to resent the program, become blind to its benefits, because they feel left out or uninformed. Share the two important most important statements (vision and mission) that serve as the program's foundation, direction, and life line with the members of the entire school (teachers, secretaries, custodians, food service personnel, maintenance personnel, aids, substitutes, assistant administrators, and volunteers) because this open sharing makes everyone have a vested interest in the program's success. This process was also the method that I used to get "buy in" from all of the players at C. E. Ellison High School. These individuals began to provide information about various student opportunities, and I welcomed their knowledge and assistance. These individuals knew that I genuinely appreciated them and their efforts to support the students of the C. E. Ellison High School Leadership Academy. New programs must remain visibly active in the whole school environment and the surrounding community in order counted as a worthwhile program by many individuals. Also important to remember is that many individuals employed within a public school system will have children of their own, or they know children that they want to share in the experience of a program like the description included here in the Equalizer: Leadership in Action book.

# Does Management Equal Leadership?

Student leadership development consequently should be based on leadership theory, otherwise individuals having undesirable leadership traits or a lack of understanding the dynamics of leadership will lead to miniature models of that particular undesirable individual. For this reason, and others, is why great care in selection for the individual that will be teaching leadership, teaching about leadership skill development, and teaching students about their development as effective leaders of the future must be the primary objective in personnel selection. There are those individuals who hold strongly to the belief that leadership is equal to management. Although an effective leader must possess some management skills to maintain order in his/her daily routines, *development of good management skills does not equate to effective leadership skill development*. As many leadership theorists have pointed out most eloquently, managers ensure that what is already in place functions efficiently by ensuring all dots and crossed lines have occurred. The leader on the other hand, is the innovator for issues of local, national, or global concern. He/she has the ability to make important discoveries using a series of a predefined success processes and finding the solutions for problematic areas of concern. Using this simplified version as a comparison between management and leadership provides a clear distinction between the two.

Not only should the distinction between management and leadership made, this distinction must also drive personnel selection for anyone who is to teach student leadership development. Another factor that must drive personnel selection is the individual's interpersonal skills. Students have an ability and keen sense of determining those adults who are sincerely interested in their growth and development versus those who operate under a pretense of doing so. My students in particular possess the ability to make this type of determination based on their learning and training on multiple levels of leadership development, and they are not easy to fool. These students have the ability to accurately and quickly assess the leadership skills of others. They also have extremely high expectations for adult leader. They often compare the level of leadership development of the adult to that of their own development. Adults who lack the ability to be sincere, honest, and open have no real chance of developing relationships with these types of students. Interpersonal relationships are important when teaching students because students need to trust the individual before they will trust information the individual is teaching. Once there exists positive, mutual respect, and a healthy interpersonal relationship between the teacher and student, the student is ready to become receptive to the information taught to them. Students will believe in their own

155

strength, abilities, and seek opportunities for growth utilizing *SEA* (synthesize, evaluate, apply) for what they learned in multiple environments.

## Hippocratic Oath for Public Education Systems

Some educational leaders have caused the public education system to develop an undesirable record of accomplishment or the image of constantly making changes in its programs before thorough research analysis has taken place. In the mean time, students, their dreams of the future, opportunities to continue to develop, and experience growth is inhibited. Changing this endless revolution of changing programs too soon needs to be one of the most seriously addressed issues that current educational leaders and policy makers seek to immediately resolve. Educational leaders and policy makers need to finally, dig deep into the confines of their minds and seek creative methods to overcome this cycle. These individuals must become willing to hear the word no and know that it does not signal negate the worth of the goals they are trying to accomplish for the public education system. I have heard no or that I cannot do this or that all of my life. That fact has not stopped me from pursuing my dreams.

Educational leaders and policy makers must also become willing to make use of non-traditional resource availability to fund new programs that show great promise for the future of today's students education. Available resources for use in today's public education facilities should be ones that can show that they have a legitimate interest in student success, have ethical values, integrity, and ones that promote student growth. The resources exist, but some may be more difficult to discover than others may. These are the acts that local, state, and national educational leaders and policy makers will need to take in order to properly fund public education. Taxes can only stretch so far, before approaching a breaking point. Developing partnerships with major corporations and organizations are just one of the many suggestions that I have about funding public education. Chief executive officers (CEO) of major organizations or post-secondary education facilities must be able to see how they will benefit before wanting to participate in such partnerships.

If educational leaders and policy makers are unwilling or unskilled in making use of the skills necessary to ensure these things are overcome, perhaps any additional personnel changes that are being considered should include putting their names and titles in the bin to be recycled. Change is inevitable. It is the duty and responsibility of those holding the educational leader and policy maker positions to stay abreast of changes that are occurring, anticipate the new direction of needs based on these changes, and then take action to resolve the issues that arise due to change. I believe that a variety of public schools problems become alleviated when the majority of educational leaders and policy makers begin to take the cause seriously. There lies a need to truly educate students in public schools more seriously. They need to stop allowing new programs testing on students with little or no evidence of the program's long-term benefits to students after the secondary level of education. It seems that funding is sometimes granted for programs simply because it may sound similar to a category in which funding is available. Perhaps a *Public Education System Hippocratic Oath* could ensure that program's present in public school systems "… do no harm…" to the growth and development of students.

Educational leaders and policy makers should invest only in programs that meet specified criteria based on what students are *becoming and doing* as the result of a program. An analysis of successful programs should be made and then provide the information to the public. Providing feedback and information sharing across public school systems is an area needing further research. Until a public school program, educational leaders, and policy makers ensure that most of the components that I have just mentioned are effective and followed through on, inadequacies in student academic achievement will not be overcome. The issue of providing American students with an education that provides them with the tools that they need to be competitive in global environments, successful in post secondary environments, and successful in the work force will continue to be a festering and painful splinter in the eye of the members of our society as a whole.

Anything less than taking actions to correct the shortcoming in public education by educational leaders and policy makers results in individuals who are willing to simply stand back in the shadows hoping that no one demands anything of them. These are the individuals who are perfectly satisfied to wait for new policies to be made, not necessarily by individuals having any type of experience in public schools, to tell them what they will do and sometimes, though frequently incomplete, how to do it. I would like to suggest that they read *Who Moved My Cheese? An Amazing Way to Deal with Change in Your Work and in Your Life* (Johnson, 1998). This simple book needs reading by these type individuals because it provides examples and the result of inaction in the face of change. A lack of real action by educational leaders and policy makers, by my definition means that have committed to no plan, idea, or method of finding solutions for those disenchanted with the performance of the public education system. Educational leaders and policy makers falling to perform in these categories should not be referred to as being leaders at all, educational or otherwise, they wear the name leader simply due to their positions. Others show them respect only because of their position or title.

Remember, when an individual has the assignment of problem identification and then can rightly hand that problem over to someone else to do the work, he/she has the simplest duty. I do not believe that this type of individual necessarily deserves to ascribe as a leader description based on my definition of leadership or idea of an effective leader. I realize that everyone must pay his/her dues of successful growth by performing some of the less desirable duties. I also realize and believe that true leaders are your problem-solvers. True leaders are capable not only problem identification, but they are also capable of developing a plan of action, identifying resource allocations, and successfully implementing of all of these components together and harmoniously accomplishing their goals and objectives.

True leaders are not just mouths full of words; they are the movers and shakers that get the job done through *Leadership in Action*. As I stated earlier, I believe that the issues of the life-long achievement and success for all students will take the concerted efforts of all educational stakeholders. We must all become proactively involved in our schools, in the lives of all children, and find the best solutions for the identified problems in public education. I hold no animosity or ill will towards the educational leaders and policy makers who are making real moves in the direction to ensure the achievement and success of students. I have had the opportunity to know educational leaders whose abilities have been unmatched to date. However, for the educational leaders and policy makers who have comfortably sat back and collected pay for inaction, continuing to do the same old things with the same old results in the midst of an environment that is constantly changing, I believe that the educational stakeholders need to demand change. Our nation and future status depends on effective changes in the public school system that has lasting results of success.

## New Beginnings

In August 2004, I received the Master of Education (M.Ed.) degree that qualified me to become an administrator in a public school setting. It was my original intent to continue providing effective student leadership development to students attending public schools within the Killeen Independent School District. I proposed the formation of a District Director of Student Leadership Development position to both Mr. Rainwater and the KISD Superintendent, Dr. Charles Patterson so that I could train other teachers to serve as coordinators using the ME and FIP-2004. This position would have been equivalent to that of an administrator. While both agreed that the position was a good idea, nothing more than positive comments ever materialized. I suspect financing a district wide move toward this type of educational revolution was the culprit causing this inaction. At the time of the proposal, I was unaware of major changes going on within the KISD. Perhaps these changes or finance were some of the reasons that the new position failed to materialize. I am still not sure.

I do not believe that the old saying, "Good things come to those who wait", is always necessarily, true. However, I do believe that if your intentions are good and your goal is to help make society better as a whole, as you begin the journey to accomplish your dreams, refuse to compromise your value and belief systems, then, and only then, will the end-result have a positive outcome. On August 30, 2004, I resigned as the C. E. Ellison High School Leadership Academy Coordinator in Killeen, Texas. On August 31, 2004, I became an administrator within the Copperas Cove Independent School District. I am currently the Senior Class Principal at Copperas Cove High School in Copperas Cove, Texas. Copperas Cove High School implemented a program approximately 10 years ago in which all teachers and administrators serve as mentors for a small group of students. All of the teachers and administrators serve as mentors teaching leadership to their assigned student groups which consists of approximately 10 to 12 students each. All students are able to participate in the training that occurs every Wednesday for 30 minutes each week. Being the usual me, I see things that I would do differently. Teachers, staff, and administrators at the Copperas Cove High School support ideas or programs that are conducive to student learning on a school wide basis. Copperas Cove High School is off to a great start in discovering the real world answer to student achievement and success.

Dr. George Willey, Principal at Copperas Cove High School, conducted research for his dissertation on teen leadership development. We share many of the same ideas about student growth and their need for leadership development. He also firmly believes in training and preparing his assistant principals with the tools that they will need to be successful as a main principal in the public school system someday. His leader development philosophy is to promote, train, and provide individuals with learning opportunities. All of this is for the purpose successfully performing the job duties as the primary leader of his/her own public school when that job opportunity arises. Dr. Willey is a leader who prepares his four assistant principal's for growth and to spread what he/she has learned from him to other environments as the primary administrator. He is a leader who not only "talks the talks, but he also walks the walk."

The students at Copperas Cove High School did not know how to take me at first, but I am getting to know the majority of them on multiple levels. Believe it, or not, I have already gained the support of a majority of teachers, other administrators, and the staff using the various mechanisms of my alternative discipline plans. I began implementing the components of alternative discipline after approximately one to two months in my new position. The alternative discipline assists the student in correcting his/her own undesirable behavior [student responsibility and accountability]. So far, the alternative discipline has the attention of the approximately 2050 students attending Copperas Cove High School. Although I do not know all of the students yet, they have quickly learned to identify me as I walk up and down the halls.   In addition to student leadership training, the alternative discipline will most likely be the topic of my next book in the future.

## Author's Note

Through various simulated scenarios, I have provided a glimpse of how my personal experiences assisted me in the formation of my theory, development of the Model of Excellence, dreams for the future, and writing the contents of this book.  I hold firm to the believe that an individual's ability to develop as a life-long learner has a direct linkage to my theory.  Student leadership development and abilities have more to do with learning through experience and opportunity than with an individual's age.  It is also my belief in training and developing high school students today, so that they can effectively serve as the future local, state, and national leaders.  In addition to my ideas, I have provided the Model of Excellence in its entirety.  I included this information hoping that my readers will share my passion for high school student leadership development, my vision of transforming the future of public education, and my plans for student leadership training's full implementation as a realistic mechanism for life-long change.  As stated by my brother Adrian during a conversation that we had about the current mind set about today's public education system, he stated, "If people aren't willing to become a part of the *solution* to the problem, then they are the *problem*."

An overall goal for my vision of transformation is to not only address the academic needs of students while in high school, but also to provide tools for a the individuals who have been assigned the task of effectively implementing programs that assist students accomplish their future goals.  When students develop the leadership skills for future successes and the ability to make sound decisions, I will be able to sleep soundly and in peace as an elderly individual.  This peaceful sound sleep will be due to the fact that I will have confidence that the decisions that directly affect me have been made by ethical leaders that possess sound skills that have assisted them in making those necessary decisions.  Remember: *Leadership is the process of developing the power to visualize future environments, a willingness to take part in planning, individual growth, and implementing necessary resources to make visions become reality.*  This is the picture of tomorrow's leaders.

## Equalizer: Leadership in Action Vision

My original vision eventually developed into one that was larger than C. E. Ellison High School Leadership Academy and even larger than the Killeen Independent School District.  My vision has become one of serving as an effective change agent for public school systems, working with teachers, administrators, educational leaders, policy makers, and other adults wanting to develop the effective leadership that will lead to a better position or pay. Serving as an effective change agent, my vision is to provide effective leadership development assistance through use of my definition of leadership, the Model of Excellence, and FIP-2004. As a matter of fact, my vision developed into one that can serve a multitude of individuals through a new consulting and motivational speaker business that I recently started doing business as (DBA) called the Equalizer: Leadership in Action (ELIA). As I stated earlier, the vision and mission statements are two of the most important aspects of an organization/business having the intent of success. The ELIA vision statement, *Equalization and Future Success through Leadership in Action* and the ELIA mission statement, *Equalizer: Leadership in Action provides the long-term solution for members of today's society as they continually strive for excellence in multifaceted aspects of their lives.*

## Specific Target Groups for ELIA

- ❖ High school students seeking to make a difference in their environments through excellence;
- ❖ High school students making poor choices that result in academic failure, negative consequences, or disciplinary action;
- ❖ Adults seeking advancement as successfully developed leaders in various job markets;
- ❖ Educational Leaders serious about the long-term development and training for tomorrow's leaders; and
- ❖ Educators wanting to truly have the ability to teach their content areas uninterrupted by issues of discipline;

Servicing these specific target groups will provide me with multiple settings and varying demographics for comparisons. Participants in the Equalizer: Leadership in Action (ELIA) Program would all have the common goal of finding situations and opportunities that enable recognition of personal strengths and power to achieve successes through many facets of their school, surrounding community, and their personal goals for the future. Beginning leadership development training at the secondary level provides greater assurance that the learned skills will become a way of life for individuals participating in the program. This may sound like a tall order to fill. Having the vision of implementing training that has a lifelong impact on individual's achievement in a variety of environments can become a realistic realty for all of us. Participants in this training will experience a paradigm shift in their current perception for the future direction of society as a whole. My research currently targets high school students, but it is easily adaptable for use in middle schools, universities, and the business world.

# Overarching National Benefits

Imagine public schools having a modified freedom to implement a student leadership development program into schools using these same concepts and methods as described in this book. I have learned that these concepts and methods are necessary to promote student success in multiple settings. Imagine the freedom, opportunities, and creativity that successful experiences will have on students throughout their lifetimes. All of these things are realistic possibilities for students attending public schools while still meeting the specific campus, district, and statewide goals and objectives for student success and achievement. Participating students under my tutelage within the C.E. Ellison High School Leadership Academy have far exceeded all anticipated expectations of all educational stakeholders (parents, educators, administrators, policy makers, students, and community members). To the educational stakeholders, imagine the endless progress and benefits to our nation that is possible in a short time by implementing such powerful training in the public school system. Imagine how such a focused face-lift in public education would change the abilities, mindsets, and dreams for the future would change the current workforce and individuals entering into higher education facilities.

Additional benefits to individuals choosing to use the Equalizer: Leadership in Action (ELIA) Program provides consistency in the evidence of improvement and program intervention. In addition to this, participants have a realistic plan in place that meets their specific needs, long-term benefits of student achievement, and the ability to continue successes in the midst of changes in environmental issues and influences. It is for this reason that I refer to effective leadership development as the equalizer in achievement, success, and lifelong learning. In spite of an individual's beginnings or environmental influences, learning and implementing the effective skills outlined in the Equalizer: Leadership in Action book provides them with the tools that are needed to successfully overcome the circumstances of which they have no or very little control. Additional benefits using the combined components (real world definition of leadership, ME, and FIP-2004) of the Equalizer: Leadership in Action program follows:

- ❖ Based on specific targeted groups of individuals;
- ❖ Based on leadership theory, development, and application of learned skills through special projects;
- ❖ Development of leadership attributes that both students and adults need to possess;
- ❖ Distinguishes and Identifies the role of both leaders and non-leaders in a team or working environment;

❖ Identifies Students Gifted in Leadership and Student Leaders;
❖ Assessment of Leadership Development;
❖ Strong Correlations between Leadership Development, Attendance, and Behavior Management for both students and adults;
❖ A life line for teachers new to the profession; and
❖ It works in a variety of environments.

## Future Direction of ELIA :

❖ Motivational Speaking at:
   1. Public middle/high schools
   2. Various higher education facilities
   3. Various businesses
❖ Consulting Services
   1. Public middle/high schools
   2. Various higher education facilities
   3. Various businesses
❖ Service and Availability for Educational Leaders and Policy Makers
❖ ELIA Summer Programs
   1. Professional Development
   2. Educational Leaders and Policy Makers
   3. Texas Education Agencies
   4. Education Service Centers
   5. Teachers
   6. Parents
   7. Students (ELIA alumni and members involved in original research)
   8. ELIA Program Coordinators
❖ Continued Research and Development
❖ Leadership Training Interactive Website

## IMPORTANT POINTS TO REMEMBER ABOUT ELIA:

1. An effective means of training individuals to get through the next preparatory steps of life that enables them to accomplish their future goals;
2. Power to accomplish greatness lies within self. For those who are unaware that they possess this power, situations and opportunities can ensure its enlightenment;
3. Educational reforms and accountability misguided focus for lasting change at national, state, and local levels have traditionally missed the mark because student *academic achievement* and *success* still "boils"

163

down to the student's willingness to be responsible for learning the material;

4. An effective method to "Close The Gap" between student academic achievement linked to ethnic, cultural, social, economic, gender and/or environmental differences;

5. Effective classroom management and assistance for individuals new to the teaching profession,

6. Prepares individuals become actively involved in their environments, and

7. Leadership is the process of developing the power to visualize future environments, a willingness to take part in planning, individual growth, and implementing necessary resources to make visions become reality.

If your organization would be interested in me serving as a leadership development consultant or motivational speaker for your school, business, state/government facility, or higher education facility, send request to the below address. Include a brief statement about your school or business, specific information about any time constraints that may exist, and describe the audience for the service. I hope readers found areas within this book that have provided some degree of enlightenment about student leadership development as key in the public education system. My hope is that all readers of the Equalizer: Leadership in Action book, are able to find portions of the book that were specific to their style, needs, and/or areas of interest.

ELIA
P.O. BOX 477
Copperas Cove, Texas 76522
afarlow@hot.rr.com
(254) 542-4195

Yours truly,
Angela J. Farlow

# Notes

**Title I, Part F of the ESEA and CSR**

Provisions of Title I, Part F of the Elementary and Secondary Education Act (ESEA) supports this idea by stating that program must have the ability or hold promise of providing rigorous evidence that is research-based to support the claims of new programs. The eleven components of the CSR further established guidelines to follow to lending support for this same idea. An adequate system of scoring that offered information about the degree to which the standards and guidelines was met for new program intervention was absent in both of these documents. Due to this absence, I developed a standard score of greater than or equal to 80% in the educational setting equates to an above average score.

**Comprehensive School Reform (CSR)**

The Comprehensive School Reform (CSR) Program began in 1998 and was authorized as Title I, Part F of the Elementary and Secondary Education Act signed into law on January 8, 2002 (TEA, n.d.). My research with the students in the C. E. Ellison High School Leadership Academy program has shown that the ability to conduct scientifically based research, provide rigorous evidence of intervention, and meet the eleven components of the federal guidelines for comprehensive school reform can be accomplished. Additionally, program effectiveness comparisons were realistically obtainable making comparisons between the goals and objectives of the Federal Guidelines for Comprehensive School Reform (CSR), NCLB, and the current practices portion for C.E. Ellison High School Leadership Academy the goals and objectives that were included in the 2003-2004 Campus Improvement Plans (CIP).

**CSR Components**

The eleven components of the federal guidelines for comprehensive school reform are as follow:

1. *Effective, research-based methods and strategies*: A comprehensive school reform program employs innovative strategies and proven methods for student learning, teaching, and school management that are based on reliable research and effective practices, and have been replicated successfully in schools with diverse characteristics.

2. *Comprehensive design with aligned components*: The program has a comprehensive design for effective school functioning, including instruction, assessment, classroom management, professional development, and parental involvement. It also includes school management that aligns the school's curriculum, technology, and professional development into a school wide reform plan designed to enable all students—including children from low-income families, children with limited English proficiency, and children with disabilities—to meet challenging State

content and performance standards. The program also addresses needs identified through a school needs assessment.

3. *Professional development*: The program provides high-quality and continuous teacher and staff professional development and training.

4. *Measurable goals and benchmarks*: A comprehensive school reform program has measurable goals for student performance tied to the state's challenging standards as well as benchmarks for meeting those performance goals.

5. *Support within the school*: school faculty, administrators, and staff support the program.

6. *Parental and community involvement*: The program provides for the meaningful involvement of parents and the local community in planning and implementing school improvement activities.

7. *External technical support and assistance*: A comprehensive reform program utilizes high-quality external support and assistance from a comprehensive school reform entity (which may be a university) with experience or expertise in school wide reform and improvement.

8. *Evaluation strategies*: The program includes a plan for the evaluation of the implementation of school reforms and the student results achieved.

9. *Coordination of resources*: The program identifies how other resources (federal, state, local, and private) available to the school will be utilized to coordinate services to support and sustain the school reform.

10. *Support for teachers, administrators, and staff*: The program provides support teachers, administrators, and other school staff.

11. *Evidence of improved academic achievement*: The program has been found to significantly improve the academic achievement of students or demonstrates strong evidence that it will improve the academic achievement of students.

**Scoring:**

An overall score of 80% (above average) or higher on all measures within the FIP-2004 package signifies success in the following areas under study: identification of the attributes of students gifted and talented in leadership program implementation, community service-based project, and program success analysis. Areas of study receiving less than 80% should become the focal point for evaluation, reflection, and modifications implemented during the following year.

**Stakeholder Survey**

The *Stakeholder Survey* addresses all eleven components of the Comprehensive School Reform (CSR). This 30-item *Stakeholder Survey* includes both a mean score and a calculated percent value for each statement. Responses for questions 02, 06, and 11 are reversed according to the following system of value as: 5 = Strongly

Disagree, 4 = Disagree, 3 = Neither Agree or Disagree, 2 = Agree, or 1 = Strongly Agree.

## Summary of Stakeholder Survey Results

Questions 2,3,6,10, 25, and 27 were the exception in receiving an overall score of 80% or higher. The resulting scores of 80% or higher occurred in 24 out of 30 total statements. All 11 components of the Federal guidelines for comprehensive school reform evaluations for the C. E. Ellison High School Leadership Academy program during the year of 2003-2004. C. E. Ellison High School Leadership Academy program effectiveness based on the 11 CSR components resulted in an overall score of 80%. According to the calculated scores and the standards established within the FIP-2004, six specific areas within 5 different areas of comprehensive school reform should become the focus for next year's (2004-2005) program improvement analysis and activities.

## Actual Scores

Questions 2,3,10, 25, and 27 overall score percentages were within the 76-78% range. Question 6 overall score percent was calculated at 69%.

## [References: Action Research Study]

Airasian, P., & Gay L. (2003). Educational research competencies for analysis and *applications* (7th ed., pp. 463-470). Upper Saddle River, New Jersey: Merrill Prentice Hall.

Bennis, W., & Goldsmith, J. (1997). Learning to lead: A workbook on becoming a leader
  (Rev. ed.). Reading, MA: Perseus Books.

Burns, J. M. (1978). *Leadership.* New York, NY: Harper & Row.

Covey, S. R. (1989). The 7 habits of highly effective people: Powerful lessons in personal change, restoring the character ethic. New York, NY: Fireside, Simon & Schuster.

Gardner, J. W. (1990). *On leadership.* New York, NY: The Free Press.

Hackman, M. Z., & Johnson, C. E. (1995). Leadership communication skills. In Wren T. J. (Ed.), The leader's companion: Insights on leadership through the ages (pp.428- 431). New York, NY: The Free Press.

Karnes, F. A., & Bean, S. M. (1995). Leadership for students: A practical guide for ages *8-18.* Waco, TX: Prufrock Press.

Lumsden, L. (1997). *Expectations for students.* Retrieved April 22, 2003, from http://eric.uoregon.edu/publications/digests/digest116.html.

Lumsden, L. (1994). *Student motivation to learn.* Retrieved April 22, 2003, from http://eric.uoregon.edu/publications/digests/digest092.html.

Maxwell, J. C. (2001). *The power of leadership.* Nashville, Tennessee: Thomas Nelson.

Maxwell, J. C. (1999). *The 21 indispensable qualities of a leader.* Nashville, Tennessee: Thomas Nelson.

Maxwell, J. C., & Ziglar, Z. (1998). *The 21 irrefutable laws of leadership: Follow them and people will follow you* (pp. 21-31). Nashville, Tennessee: Thomas Nelson.

Noteboom, S. (Speaker). (2002). *Response to interview questions.* (Cassette Recording No. 1). Killeen, TX: Angela Farlow.

Payne, R. (1998). *A framework for understanding poverty.* (Rev.ed.). Baytown, TX: RFT Publishing.

Rainwater, M. (Speaker). (2002). *Response to interview questions.* (Cassette Recording No. 2). Killeen, TX: Angela Farlow.

Smith, R. B. (1995). Talent and training for leadership. In Wren T. J. (Ed.), *The leader's companion: Insights on leadership through the ages* (pp.464-471). New York, NY: The Free Press.

Texas Education Agency. (n.d.). 2002 *Academic Excellence Indicator System.* Retrieved April 22, 2002, from http://www.tea.state.tx.us.

United States Government. (2002). *No child left behind.* Retrieved on April 11, 2002 from http://www.nochildleftbehind.gov/next/overview/index.html

**C. E. Ellison High School Leadership Academy Performance Objectives**

Current Practices

CIP –Page 13

Name of campus: C. E. Ellison High School

Current Practice: Current practices directed at improving achievement include a number of specific programs and processes directly related to student progress.

7. Leadership Academy

The Leadership Academy at Ellison High School continues to provide an educational program that empowers teachers and students by providing them with real world applications for a lifelong learning experience, develops student leadership skills and qualities, fosters higher standards of academic achievement, and helps students to achieve future success regardless of their area of interest. The Academy will provide an avenue for partnerships with business and community leaders to become more involved at Ellison and positively influence student success.

**CIP –Page 13 Campus Improvement Plan Results**

❖ Leadership Academy Board of Directors composed of community leaders, business owners, and parents established in August 2003.

❖ The members of the Board of Directors attended monthly meeting, taught theme topics to members and staff during meeting, were instrumental in giving students feedback during project proposals, and they were able to interact with these students on a professional level.

- ❖ The members of the Board of Directors were also instrumental in gaining community leader support for the Leadership Academy through their conversations about the program and their willingness to select members for high profile community opportunities and duties.

- ❖ Partnerships established with the International Rotary Evening and Morning clubs through information presentations conducted by Mrs. Farlow.  This positive encounters later lead to members receiving scholarships and opportunities to attend the youth RYLA summer leadership training camps.  Partnership establishment with the West Point Society selected the Leadership Academy as its representative organization within the school.  Member Lenna Black became the first member to receive the Leadership Award for 2003-2004.  Presentations at the Lion's Evening and Noon clubs, which provided additional opportunities for Leadership Academy members.

- ❖ Due to some type of issues as stated by Mr. Rainwater, the  GB 1033 Business and Society Leadership Focus Course taught at C. E. Ellison High School by Tarleton State University –Central Texas professors again.

**CIP –Page 17**

By the end of the school year 2004, 80% of students in all subgroups will pass the initial Texas Assessment of Knowledge and Skills (TAKS) test.

1. To increase the involvement of parents and community in the educational process.

To implement professional development programs, which promote teacher growth and meet student needs.

By the end of the school year 2004, senior SAT/PSAT/ACT scores and participants will increase.

To improve student academic success by increasing attendance and lowering the dropout rate.

To provide a safe, positive learning environment for students and staff.

By the end of the school year 2004, Advanced Placement test scores will increase.

**CIP –Page 17 Campus Improvement Plan Results**

1. All members of the Leadership Academy passed all portions of the Texas Assessment of Knowledge and Skills (TAKS) test.  Several members received one, two, or three ratings in the commendable category.  Additionally, some of the members received a commendable rating in all four categories.

2. Professional development programs, which promote teacher growth and meet student needs Mrs. Farlow continued her graduate courses which allowed Leadership Academy members to benefit as she implemented

169

various components for her graduate school courses. Robert Marshall continued to serve as a professor for Tarleton State University.

3. Senior SAT/PSAT/ACT scores are expected to become available after the time of this report. Leadership Academy members received scores of 2, 3, and 4 on several Advanced Placement tests across on disciplines.

**Summary:**

Some of the information such as the items in 5 and 6 are the responsibility of the entire school personnel. Attendance rates expect to remain at or above the 95 % rate as in previous years. C. E. Ellison High School is a safe school and in the state PEIMS report.

**Form CIP-1, Goal # 3 Objective # 1 Activity # 8**

**CIP –Page 32**

2. Performance objective #1: By the end of the school year 2004, 80% of students in all subgroups will pass the initial Texas Assessment of Knowledge and Skills (TAKS) test.

3. Program activity/strategy # 8: Leadership Academy Peer Tutoring

4. Beginning date: August 18, 2003 Ending date: May 28, 2004

Person(s) responsible: Angela Farlow- Leadership Academy Coordinator

Leadership Academy Site Team Members Killeen Independent School District 2002-2003 Campus Improvement Plan

Campus Program Description

Name of campus: C. E. Ellison High School

1. District goal #3: Student achievement: Improve academic performance through the continued development of instructional strategies, which promote excellence; methods, which accommodate transitions, and systems, designed to meet the needs of individual students.

5. Description of program activity/strategy (activity, resources, and related staff development): Leadership Academy students will offer peer tutoring in the library on Monday evenings from 4:00-6:00 to all students. Tutoring will also is available based on teacher referrals.

6. Program area(s) involved in this activity (x):

Technology (X) G/T (X) ESL (X) Special Ed (X)

Dropout Reduction (X)

7. Budget information for special programs (where applicable)

8. Evaluation plan for this program activity (formative/incremental evaluation):

*TAKS results- 80% in all subgroups

*Decrease in failure rates among students that received tutoring.

*Increase in grade average for content area that received tutoring.

*Sign-in sheets to track participation.

170

**CIP –Page 32 Campus Improvement Plan Results**

1. Leadership Academy Peer Tutoring:

Salwa Yordi and Yeraldin Yordi, junior and senior members of the Leadership Academy provided tutoring for the ESL students during the entire 2003-2004 school year. Tutoring consisted of translation of information and instructions in Spanish to students, research assistance, specific content areas such as math, biology, English, World Geography, Spanish for those students whose primary language was not the Spanish language, and final exams.

2. Chemistry tutoring provided on an "as needed" basis. Mrs. Torres (ESL) teacher brought her students down to receive tutoring from members or the Leadership Academy Coordinator in room 133.

3. All members of the Leadership Academy passed all portions of the Texas Assessment of Knowledge and Skills (TAKS) test. Several members received one, two, or three ratings in the commendable category. Additionally, some of the members received a commendable rating in all four categories.

4. Leadership Academy members received scores of 2, 3, and 4 on several Advanced Placement tests across on disciplines.

**Summary:**

The peer-tutoring concept was not widely supported by the teachers at C. E. Ellison High School by providing the Leadership Academy Coordinator with the names of students needing additional academic assistance. As a result, only a minority population of students benefited from the Peer-Tutoring portion of the program (see 1 and 2 in this section).

**Form CIP-1, Goal # 4 Objective # 2 Activity #2**

**CIP –Page 38**

Killeen Independent School District 2003-2004 Campus Improvement Plan
Campus Program Description
Name of campus: C. E. Ellison High School

1. District goal # 4: Maintain parental and community involvement programs which promote the academic, social, and emotional growth of students.

2. Performance objective # 2: To increase the involvement of parents and community in the educational process.

3. Program activity/strategy #1: Community partnership

4. Beginning date: August 18, 2003 Ending date: May 27, 2004

5. Person(s) Responsible: Angela Farlow- Leadership Academy Coordinator

a. Leadership Academy Site Team Members

b. Leadership Academy Board of Directors

**Description of program activity/strategy (activity, resources, and related staff development):**

171

Leadership Academy students will complete projects that will positively change the culture, climate, and environment of C. E. Ellison High School. A Board of Directors, consisting of community leaders, and provide feedback on member academy projects, community relations, and the development of interpersonal skills. Tarleton University will collaborate with the Leadership Academy to provide the GB 1033 Business and Society Leadership Focus Course to Ellison students.

6. Program area(s) involved in this activity (x):

Technology (X) Career Education (X) Discipline Management (X)

Dropout Reduction (X)

7. Budget information for special programs (where applicable)

8. Budget Amounts: 6100: $ 3,200 6200: $ 6300: $ 6400: $

Evaluation plan for this program activity (include formative/incremental evaluation)

*Surveys to determine the programs effectiveness

*The number of junior/senior community service projects completed and presented will increase from less than or equal to 8 up to approximately 15. Data analysis for each project will be compiled, recorded, and stored for future use.

*Number of students participating and completing the Tarleton Leadership class.

*Students' grades and credit received from class compilation for future data.

**CIP –Page 38 Campus Improvement Plan Results**

Survey comparisons to determine the programs effectiveness: The following surveys were developed by Angela J. Farlow, coordinator of the C. E. Ellison High School Leadership Academy, to be used in her independent and ongoing personal student leadership development research. However, she used several of the surveys that she had developed during her original thesis research. Use of these surveys are intended to determine the C. E. Ellison High School Leadership Academy's program effectiveness and the programs ability to meet the 11 components of CSR.

❖ Stakeholder Survey Results
❖ Leadership in Action
❖ Project Success Analysis Survey
❖ Training Seminar Survey
❖ 2004 Project Symposium Survey

1. Number of junior/senior projects:

The number of Junior/Senior projects completed and presented will increase from 8 to 2. Data analysis for each project was completed. During the 2003-2004 school year, the traditional senior projects now include sophomore and junior members. The following list includes all completed projects by member classification.

17 total projects were completed however one sophomore member declined to present at the time of the 2004 Project Symposium. 16 projects were actually presented.

a. Seniors = 4

b. Juniors = 7

c. Sophomores = 5

Data analysis on each project has been recorded, documented, preserved in member's personal electronic portfolios, notebooks to serve as examples for upcoming members, and compact disk kept on file in the Leadership Academy database.

2. Number of students participating and completing the Tarleton State University

     a. 3-hour college credit course

     b. 16 Students enrolled in the GB 1033 Business and Society Leadership Focus Course.

     c. 13 students completed the course and received college credit.

     d. The completion rate for the college credit course is 81.3 %

**Summary:**

Dr. Malone, a professor at Tarleton State University, conducted survey with the Students that completed the course and shared the results with Mrs. Farlow. The results of the survey showed an overall approval rating for the course and student performance and expectation clarity. Most of the student survey responses gave an overall approval rating for the focused leadership training learning, goals, and objectives. One area the surveyed students cited, as an area of needing improvement was that one professor should teach the entire course. Students stated that the leadership styles and expectations were too different.

3. Leadership Academy Board of Directors composed of community leaders, business owners, and parents established in August 2003.

4. Leadership Academy students completed all senior project requirements:

The Cultural Exchange; Ellison High School Marquee Project; 2004 B.A.E.H. Youth Leadership Conference and B.A.E.H. Scholarship Fund; David Lubar Author's Visit; Heart of Texas Discovery; Building Blocks to the Future; National Ambassador Experience; Ellison High School vs. Temple High School Blood Drive; The Eagle Eyes On the Future; The Emerald's Little Gems. All of these projects were specific to the positive changes that occurred in the culture, climate, and environment of C. E. Ellison High School. The collected data and project information kept in room 133 for future reference.

## Attributes of Students Leaders and Students Gifted and Talented in Leadership

    1. Vision –refers to a clearly articulated and attractive alternative to the current state, situation, or cause.

2. Passion –refers to an individual's unwavering enthusiasm toward an activity, object, or concept.

3. Mission –refers to one's ability to state the core values and the core purpose of his/her activities or projects.

4. Compassion –refers to one's ability to sympathize with other's shortcomings or situations and a willingness to become involved to develop solutions to rectify them.

5. Reflection –refers the ability to identify his/her strengths and weaknesses as related to attaining higher levels of academic success.

6. Perseverance –refers to persistence in the attainment of a goal even when faced by adversity or challenging obstacles.

7. Empathy –refers to the capacity of an individual to tune into or vicariously experience another's feelings, thoughts, or experiences.

8. New Creations –refers to the desire to create new ideas in a changing environment.

9. Futuristic Perspective –refers an individual's ability to visualize future environments

10. Success –refers to the degree to which an individual accomplishes his/her desired goal.

11. Intrinsic Motivation –refers to the force that drives an individual's action and specific behavior exhibited to accomplish a goal essentially becomes internalized.

12. Accountability –refers to an individual's ability to accomplish specific goals that he/she has stated without blaming others for falling short.

**[References: FIP-2004]**

Texas Education Agency (1995). *Student assessment division*. Retrieved February 5, 2004, from http://www.tea.state.tx.us/student.assessment/

Texas Education Agency (n.d.). U.S. department of education: Draft guidance on the comprehensive school reform program. Retrieved February 27, 2004, from http://www.tea.state.tx.us/nclb/usde/CSRguid02.pdf#xml=http://www.tea.state.tx.uswww.tea.state.tx.us/

# Two-Step Success Formula through Leadership in Action

| Two-Step Success Formula Through Leadership in Action | |
|---|---|
| **STEP 1** | |
| SLD | Student Leadership Development |
| ME | Model of Excellence |
| FIP-2004 | Farlow Instrument Package –2004 |
| $\Delta P$ | Change in Perception |
| **STEP 2** | |
| P | Community Service-Based Project |
| Ex | Striving to Achieve Academic Best |
| SDL | Self-Directed Learners |
| LLL | Life-Long Learners |
| **RESULT** | |
| Contributing Citizens | Future Leaders |

## C. E. Ellison High School Leadership Academy
## 2003 –2004 Historical First

❖ Clearly articulated goals and objectives through development of Vision and Mission Statements

❖ Senior projects: Expanded to include sophomore and junior members.

❖ Meredith Kliewer "Leading the Way" as the first junior to complete the traditionally senior project.

❖ Board of Directors established consisting of active community leaders in Killeen, Texas.

❖ Tarleton State University in Central Texas, Leadership Focus, Business and Society, GB 1033, 3-semester hour college credit course.

❖ Members serving as C. E. Ellison High School Leadership Academy Ambassadors at National Leadership Conferences: Washington, D.C., New York, Florida, California, Illinois, and Texas, and during the summer.

❖ New Leadership Academy Logo

❖ Member as NASA Program Participant

❖ Official Colors (Green and Purple)

❖ Program presentations at 2004 National Association of African American Studies and 2004 Texas Association of Gifted and Talented Leadership Conference

❖ Member recognized by the National Association of Secondary School

- Principals (NASSP) for community service contributions.
- Member recognized and received a scholarship from the National Association of Secondary School Principals (NASSP) for implementing a project that provided a service to the community.

## Senior Project Score Results

### Null Hypothesis Tests

There were 41 total 2004 Project Symposium Surveys from both non-member and member participants. Senior member project scores were based on a greater than or equal to 80 percent value to receive a success rating. Four different series of test were ran on the collected data from the participant survey results for senior members that completed all components of the program. The first test conducted was a null hypothesis test analysis. Using a series of calculations that would lead to either accepting or rejecting the null hypothesis statement, comparisons between students A, B, C, and D scores for analysis took place. A comparison between students A and students B scores established that the overall project score of students A were the highest. The other comparisons used the scores from student B, the second highest score. The null hypothesis statement: While there may be a difference in the scores, these differences are not significant.

### Null Hypothesis Test Results

| Comparison # 1 | Comparison # 2 | Comparison # 3 |
|---|---|---|
| Students A and Students B | Students B and Students C | Students B and Students D |
| t = .333 | t = 3.23 | t = 10.60 |
| $\alpha$ = .05 | $\alpha$ = .05 | $\alpha$ = .05 |
| df = 9 | df = 9 | df = 9 |
| t Table value = 2.62 | t Table value = 2.62 | t Table value = 2.62 |
| Accept the Null Hypothesis | Reject the Null Hypothesis | Reject the Null Hypothesis |

Second, a series of calculations for the standard z score analysis took place. Standard z scores use both negative and positive values and the graphic visuals provide a clear interpretation analysis between score differences.

### Standard z Scores

| $z = X - \mu/\sigma$ | zQ1 | zQ2 | zQ3 | zQ4 | zQ5 |
|---|---|---|---|---|---|
| Student A | 0.54 | 0.41 | 0.57 | 1.17 | 0.56 |
| Student B | 0.76 | 1.18 | 0.66 | 0.17 | 0.45 |
| Student C | 0.15 | -0.48 | 0.22 | -0.09 | 0.51 |
| Student D | -1.45 | -1.09 | -1.47 | -1.26 | -1.5 |
| $z = X - \mu/\sigma$ | zQ6 | zQ7 | zQ8 | zQ9 | zQ10 |
| Student A | 0.78 | 0.12 | 1.06 | 0.93 | 0.49 |
| Student B | 0.48 | 0.18 | 0.55 | 0.39 | 0.85 |
| Student C | 0.17 | 0.14 | -0.1 | 0.07 | 0.1 |
| Student D | -1.45 | -0.45 | -1.5 | -1.41 | -1.43 |

## Standard z Score Graph #1

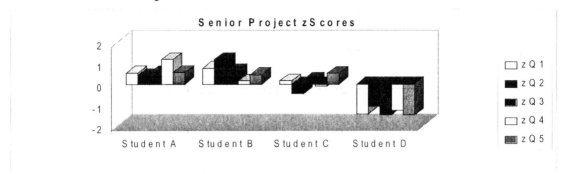

## Standard z Score Graph #2

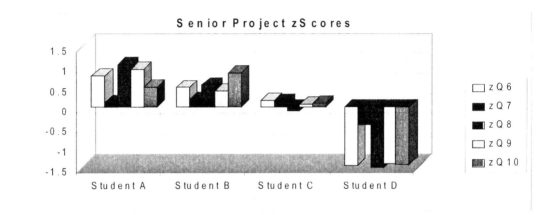

The third test conducted was a t-Test variance comparison. Selection of the t-Test used the same format of students A and B, students B and C, and students B and D for comparisons, and the assumed that everything else was equal. In addition to the t-Test information, descriptive analysis was also included in this series of test.

**t-Test: Two-Sample Assuming Equal Variances**

| t-Test Comparison #1, #2, and #3 | Student A | Student B | Student C | Student D |
|---|---|---|---|---|
| Mean | 4.307 | 4.265 | 3.822 | 2.492 |
| Variance | 0.165867778 | 0.156583333 | 0.254396 | 0.12204 |
| Observations | 10 | 10 | 10 | 10 |
| Pooled Variance | 0.161225556 | 0.205489444 | | |
| Hypothesized M Diff. | 0 | 0 | | |
| df | 18 | 18 | | |
| t Stat | 0.233893068 | 2.185213976 | | |
| P(T<=t) one-tail | 0.408853766 | 0.021168183 | | |
| t Critical one-tail | 1.734063062 | 1.734063062 | | |
| P(T<=t) two-tail | 0.817707532 | 0.042336365 | | |
| t Critical two-tail | 2.100923666 | 2.100923666 | | |

177

**Descriptive Analysis**

|  | Student A | Student B | Student C | Student D |
|---|---|---|---|---|
| Mean | 4.307 | 4.265 | 3.822 | 2.492 |
| Standard Error | 0.12879 | 0.125133 | 0.1594978 | 0.1104717 |
| Median | 4.45 | 4.29 | 4 | 2.515 |
| Mode | 4.56 | 4.29 | #N/A | 2.39 |
| Standard Deviation | 0.407269 | 0.395706 | 0.5043764 | 0.3493422 |
| Sample Variance | 0.165868 | 0.156583 | 0.2543956 | 0.12204 |
| Kurtosis | -0.254691 | 4.928873 | 0.7816282 | 2.257907 |
| Skewness | -0.641822 | -1.87517 | -1.2505687 | 0.165029 |
| Range | 1.31 | 1.44 | 1.56 | 1.37 |
| Minimum | 3.59 | 3.27 | 2.78 | 1.83 |
| Maximum | 4.9 | 4.71 | 4.34 | 3.2 |
| Sum | 43.07 | 42.65 | 38.22 | 24.92 |
| Count | 10 | 10 | 10 | 10 |
| Confidence Level (95.0%) | 0.291343 | 0.283071 | 0.3608094 | 0.2499046 |

The final series of test conducted used the Model of Excellence variables (student leadership development (SDL), project (P), self-efficacy (SE), self-regulation (SR), intrinsic motivation (IM), self-directed learner (SDL), and excellence (EX) for comparisons. Comparisons made used the same student formats as found in the other tests. Determination of individual means for all seven variables for students A, B, C, and D took place. Next, a determination for the group (students A, B, C, and D) mean score calculations for each of the seven variables for were grouped together and a single mean for later comparisons was determined. Using the individual mean values for each student minus the Model of Excellence mean showed the value that each student needed to receive the maximum possible score. Each student's percent score for the Model of Excellence variable was determined using their individual mean scores divided by seven and divided again by the ME mean.

**Model of Excellence Results**

| ME | SLD | P | SE | SR | IM | SDL | EX | Indiv. M | Indiv. M − M ET | ME % T |
|---|---|---|---|---|---|---|---|---|---|---|
| Student A | 5 | 2 | 3 | 4 | 3 | 3 | 3 | 3.286 | 0.58 | 0.9204 |
| Student B | 4 | 3 | 4 | 4 | 3 | 2 | 3 | 3.286 | 0.58 | 0.9204 |
| Student C | 3 | 3 | 3 | 3 | 2 | 2 | 2 | 2.571 | -0.14 | 0.7203 |
| Student D | 2 | 1 | 2 | 2 | 2 | 1 | 2 | 1.714 | -1 | 0.4802 |
| | | | | | | | | | | |
| Mean | 3.5 | 2.25 | 3 | 3.25 | 2.5 | 2 | 2.5 | 2.714 | | |
| Model Total | 5 | 3 | 4 | 4 | 3 | 3 | 3 | 3.571 | | |
| M = Mean | | | | | | | | | | |
| T = Total | | | | | | | | | | |

**Summary of Results**

Selection as new members for students A, B, C, and D of the C. E. Ellison High School Leadership Academy occurred during the spring semester of 2003. These students did not begin any type of student leadership development as members of the program until August of 2003 during their senior year. These newest members completed all aspects of the program. In the past, no junior selections for membership took place during the spring semester before a student's senior year due to the following:

❖ Fitting the mandatory Principles of Leadership course into the senior year class schedules;

❖ 50 annual community service hours; and

❖ Various other demands placed on students during their senior year as they planned for their futures.

Some of the senior members having been members since their sophomore year had became disenchanted due to the program's past, and they were no longer actively involved. Some of the same previous members were unaware of the changes (actual student leadership development based on leadership theories, additional leadership training opportunities, vision, mission, and the program's focus) that were taking place for members in 2003-2004. Some of the previous senior members attempted to complete senior projects, but they lacked the time or passion to follow-through. These students also found it difficult to meet the established deadlines for the community service based project completion.

**Differences in Students A, B, C, and D Scores**

I cite three reasons for the differences in the community service based project scores that were the result of the various tests. The first difference may be in the level of student leadership development of the twelve attributes of students gifted and talented in leadership or student leaders.   A second difference could be that the final product and delivery of a community service based project is a valuable indicator of students who are gifted and talented in leadership or student leaders. Finally, the third difference may indicate that the community service based project completion and student leadership development should take place before a student's senior year.   Areas of student leadership development as determined through multiple year testing results gives the program coordinator opportunities to assist the student's underdeveloped areas and individualized training can become "tailored" to the needs of the individual's development.

# REFERENCES

Airasian, P., & Gay L. (2003). Educational research competencies for analysis and *applications* (7th ed., pp. 409-411 & 463-470). Upper Saddle River, New Jersey: Merrill

Prentice Hall.

Alexander, K., & Alexander M. (2001). *American public school law* (5th ed.). Belmont, California: Wadsworth Group.

Banks, J. A. (2002). *An introduction to multicultural education* (3rd ed., pp. 40-46, 58-59). Seattle, WA: Allyn & Bacon.

Beach, D., & Reinhartz, J. (2000). *Supervisory leadership: Focus on instruction* (pp. 48-49). Boston: Allyn & Bacon.

Bennis, W. (2003). On becoming a leader: The leadership classic updated and expanded (pp. 47, 117). New Boston: Perseus Books.

Bennis, B., & Goldsmith, J. (1997). Learning to lead: A workbook on becoming a leader (pp.71- 81,101, 161). (updated edition). Boston: Perseus Books.

Boehner, J. (2002, July 24). *Committee on education and the workforce.* Retrieved on September 10, 2003. from http://www.edworkforce.house.gov/index.htm

Boeree, C. G. (2003). Abraham maslow. Retrieved on November 29, 2003, from http://www.ship.edu/~cgboeree/maslow.html

Burns, J. M. (1978). *Leadership* (pp. 22, 251, 425-430). New York: Harper & Row.

Canter,L. & Canter, M. (2001). Assertive discipline: Positive behavior management for today's classroom (3rd ed.). Los Angeles, CA: Canter& Associates, Inc. (pp. 3-10).

Cicchinelli, L. & Barley, Z. (1999). Comprehensive school reform: An Evaluation guide for districts and schools. Retrieved February 29, 2004, from http://www.mcrel.ort/csrd/evalguide.pdf

CSR Practitioner's Guide to Scientifically Based Research (2003). http://www.goodschools.gwu.cdu/about_csr/index.html#Eleven. *CSR practitioner's guide to sbr – sbr & the components.* Retrieved February 29, 2004, from National Clearinghouse for Comprehensive School Reform Website: http://www.goodschools.gwu.edu/pubs/pg/components.htm

Covey, S. R. (1989). The 7 habits of highly effective people: Powerful lessons in personal change, restoring the character ethic(95-144). New York, NY: Fireside, Simon & Schuster.

Daft, R. L. (2001). *Organization theory and design* (7th ed., pp. 52-53). Cincinnati, Ohio: South-Western College Publishing.

Davis, D., & Sorrell, J. (1995, December). *Mastery learning in public schools*. Paper prepared for PSY 702: Conditions of Learning. Valdosta, GA: Valdosta State University. Available online: [http://chiron.valdosta.edu/whuitt/files/mastlear.html ]. Retrieved on April 21, 2004, from http://teach.valdosta.edu/whuitt/files/mastlear.html

Dewey, J. (1916). *Democracy and education.* Retrieved March 15, 2004, from http://www.infed.org/archives/e-texts/e-dewey7.htm

Farris, A. (Speaker). (2004). Leadership is a verb. 2004 B.A.E.H. Youth Leadership Conference in Killeen, Texas.

Future Problem Solving Program. (n.d.). Retrieved April 22, 2004 from www.fpsp.org/.

Gardner, H. (2003). [Multiple intelligences after twenty years]. Paper presented at the American Educational Research Association, Chicago, Illinois, April 21, 2003. Retrieved on April 21, 2004 from, http://pzweb.harvard.edu/PIs/HG_MI_after_20_years.pdf

Greater Killeen Chamber of Commerce. (2003). *Education.* Retrieved February 29, 2004 from http://www.gkcc.com/education.html

Greater Killeen Chamber of Commerce. (2003). *History of Killeen.* Retrieved February 29, 2004 from http://www.gkcc.com/history.html

Green, R. L. (2001). Practicing the art of leadership: A problem-based approach to implementing the isllc standards. New Jersey: Prentice-Hall, Inc.

Hackman, M. Z., & Johnson, C. E. (1995). Leadership communication skills. In Wren T. J. (Ed.), The leader's companion: Insights on leadership through the ages (pp.428-431). New York, NY: The Free Press.

Hébert, T. P., Cramond, B., Millar, G., & Silvian, A. F. (2002). *E. Paul Torrance: His life, accomplishments, and legacy* (RM02152). Storrs, CT: The National Research Center on the Gifted and Talented, University of Connecticut.

Jackson, T., Fritch, A., Nagasaka, T., & Pope, L. (2003). Procrastination and perceptions of past, present, and future. *Individual Differences Research*, 1(*1*), (17-28). Superior: University of Wisconsin, Department of Psychology.

Johnson, S. (1998). Who moved my cheese?: An a-mazing way to deal with change in your work and in your life. New York: Penguin Putnam Inc.

Jones, D. (n.d.). *What Is PBL?* Retrieved on April 21, 2004 from, http://edweb.sdsu.edu/clrit/learningtree/PBL/WhatisPBL.html.

Kanungo, R. N. & Mendonca, M. (1996). *Ethical dimensions of leadership* (pp. 89, 95-96). Thousand Oaks, California: Sage Publications, Inc.

Karnes, F. A., & Bean, S. M. (1995). Leadership for students: A practical guide for ages 8-18 (pp. 7-10). Waco, Texas: Prufrock Press.

Karnes, F. A., & Bean, S. M. (1990). Developing Leadership in Gifted Youth. ERIC EC Digest #E485. Council for Exceptional Children, Reston, Va.; ERIC Clearinghouse on Disabilities and Gifted Education, Reston, Va. Retrieved May 15, 2004 from http://www.kidsource.com/ kidsource/content/leadership_and_gifted.html

Killeen Independent School District. (2003). 2003-2004 Campus improvement plan campus program description (pp. 13,17, 32,and 38). Retrieved February 29, 2004 from http://www.killeenisd.org/ellison/EllisonHS-CampusPlan-2003-04.pdf

Koslowski, B. & Condry, J. (1977). *Can education be made intrinsically interesting to children?* (Report No. PS009843). (ERIC Document Reproduction Service No. ED152706)

Kouzes, J. & Posner, B. (1997). The leadership challenge: How to keep getting *extraordinary things done in organizations* (2nd ed., pp. 200). San Francisco, CA: Jossey- Bass Inc.

Lussier, R. N., & Achua, C. F. (2004). Leadership: Theory, application, skill development (2nd ed.). Eagan, Minnesota: Thomson-West (p. 5, 10).

Martinez-Pons, M. (2002). Parental influences on children's academic self-regulatory development [Electronic Version]. *Theory into Practice*, 41, (2), p126.

Maxwell, J. C., & Ziglar, Z. (1998). *The 21 irrefutable laws of leadership: Follow them and people will follow you.* Nashville, Tennessee: Thomas Nelson.

*Merriam-Webster's Collegiate Dictionary* (10th ed.). (1999). Springfield, MA: Merriam-Webster.

Miller, P. H. (2002). *Theories of developmental psychology* (4th ed.). New York: Worth Publishers. (pp. 48, 187-191, 323 ).

Murray, B. (2000). Teaching students how to learn. *Monitor on Psychology*, 31, (6). Retrieved October 29, 2003, from http://www.apa.org/monitor/jun00/how to learn.html

National Commission on Excellence in Education. (1983). A nation at risk. Retrieved on October 7, 2003, from http://www.ed.gov/pubs/NatAtRisk/into.html

Noteboom, S. (Speaker). (2002). *Response to interview questions.* (Cassette Recording No. 1). Killeen, TX: Angela Farlow.

Patrick, B. C., Hisley, J., Kempler, T. & College, G. (2000). What's everybody so excited about: The effects of teacher enthusiasm on student intrinsic motivation and vitality [Electronic Version]. *Journal of Experimental Education*, 68, (3), p217.

Rainwater, M. (Speaker). (2002). *Response to interview questions.* (Cassette Recording No. 2). Killeen, TX: Angela Farlow.

Renzulli, J. S. (1998). *Three-Ring Conception of Giftedness.* In Baum, S. M., Reis, S. M., & Maxfield, L. R. (Eds.). (1998). Nurturing the gifts and talents of primary grade students. Mansfield Center, CT: Creative Learning Press. Retrieved on March 12, 2004, from http://sp.uconn.edu/~nrcgt/sem/semart13.html

Rosenbaum, J. E. (2004). It's time to tell the kids: If you don't do well in high school, you won't do well in college (or on the job). *American Educator*, Spring (pp. 8-10).

Roth, W. G. (1985). Treatment implication derived from self-efficacy research with children (Report No. CG019361). Doctor of Psychology Research Paper. (ERIC Document Reproduction Service No. ED273897).

Senge, P. M. (1990). The fifth discipline: The art and practice of the learning organization. New York: Doubleday, (p. 7-8,148, 340, 358-359).

Schunk, D. H. (2001). *Self-regulation through goal setting* (Contract No. R189002001). (ERIC Document Reproduction Service No. ED462671).

Smith, R. B. (1995). Talent and training for leadership. In Wren T. J. (Ed.), *The leader's companion: Insights on leadership through the ages* (pp.464-471). New York, NY: The Free Press.

Snowden, P. E., & Gorton, R. A. (2002). *School leadership & administration: Important concepts, case studies & simulations* (6th ed., p. 73). New York: McGraw-Hill.

Taba, H. (2001). Current conceptions of the function of the school. In Schultz, F. (Ed.) *Sources: Notable selections in education* (3rd Ed., pp. 120-130). Guilford, CT: McGraw-Hill/Dushkin.

Texas Education Agency (1995). *Student assessment division.* Retrieved February 5, 2004, from http://www.tea.state.tx.us/student.assessment/

Texas Education Agency (2002). *U.S. department of education: Draft guidance on the comprehensive school reform program.* Retrieved February 27, 2004, from http://www.tea.state.tx.us/nclb/usde/CSRguid02.pdf#xml=http://www.tea.state.tx.us www.tea.state.tx.us/

Torrance, Paul.(n.d.). *Paul Torrance's Taxonomy of Creative Thinking.* Retrieved on April 22, 2004, from, http://www.cobbk12.org/~mtbethel/Classes/target/Torrance.htm

U.S. Department of Education. (n.d.). *Elementary & secondary education: No child left behind act of 2001.* Retrieved February 29, 2004, from http://www.ed.gov/policy/elsec/leg/esea02/107-110.pdf

U.S. Department of Education. (n.d.). *Part f – Comprehensive school reform.* Retrieved February 29, 2004, from http://www.ed.gov/policy/elsec/leg/esea02/pg13/html

U.S. Department of Education. (n.d.). *The eleven components.* Retrieved February 27, 2004, from http://www.ed.gov/programs/compreform/csrdoverview/edlite-sld005.html

United States Government. (2002). *No child left behind.* Retrieved on September 10, 2003, from http://www.nochildleftbehind.gov/next/overview/index.html

Wren T.J. (Ed.), The leader's companion: Insights on leadership through the ages. New York, NY: The Free Press.